Don't Africa Me

'Their' geo-branding war, 'Our' trade, tourism wounds, and Winning like China

C. P. Eze

Expert*z* in Print

ISBN-13: 978-0-9800768-0-6
ISBN-10: 0-9800768-0-3

Library of Congress Control Number:
2007939460

Author's websites: www.paschalezemedia.com,
www.exportzoom.com

Expertz in Print

What others are saying about
Don't Africa Me

"*Don't Africa Me* is eye-opening, hard-hitting and helpful."
— Falanga Sula, award-winning humanitarian, HomelandCare.org

"Paschal's book fantastically brings to the fore how ignorant and uninformed we sometimes are about Africa, and how we erroneously draw conclusions about the continent without getting the facts or even visiting it."
— Sesto Giovanni Castagnoli, Founder / President, World Spirit Forum, Zurich, Switzerland

"You may not agree entirely with Paschal but you will certainly give it to him that he is resplendently challenging and convincing. Don't Africa Me is a bold, different and systematic discourse on strategic marketing and city and nation re-branding."
— Prince Chidi Bob Ezumah, President / Founder, Africa Means Business, Minnesota

"The book is an African renaissance, and like a sword, it pierces through every stigma about the continent. This is a major geo-political literature that is bound to fascinate anyone seeking to understand

iii

one of the most complex and often misunderstood continents in the world."
— **Bankole Thompson, Senior Editor Michigan Chronicle Detroit and author of** *A Matter of Black Transformation*

"Tourism is a global industry and I know African countries have great tourism products as the author clearly contends in this book."
— **Juergen Thomas Steinmetz, Founder / Chairman, International Council of Tourism Partners, and eTurboNews, Hawaii**

"*Don't Africa Me* could be too hot to handle as some readers will discover."
— **Kyrian Nwagwu, First African-born elected official in Michigan**

Go on and claim your $99 power bonus now!

Dear Friend,

One thing is certain: You love good books but you also love good deals. That's why, when you buy this well researched and well endorsed book, I will send you my $99 premium bonus loaded with useful tips and tools, and you will get it absolutely FREE.

This is not just because I know you love good deals. It is also because I know most book lovers like you are authors-in-waiting. An author is first and foremost a book lover. So, if you are tired of being an author-in-waiting or you are already an author of a low impact book, my $99 bonus is the bracing tonic you need now to become a powerful author. I believe a segment of the world population urgently needs to gain from your perspective on an issue of interest and relevance.

Yes, I will quickly send you my premium workshop on **"Writing Your Own Powerful Book in 54 Days or Less"** absolutely FREE so you can, in the comfort of your own home or office, launch yourself on the path of becoming a powerful author without delay.

All you have to do to get this $99 bonus is: simply forward the receipt you got when you bought **_Don't Africa Me_** to paashanbooks@mail.com, with "$99 Premium Book Writing Workshop Bonus" as subject line, and I will send you the premium workshop FREE of Charge because I believe you have a good book in you that cannot wait any longer.

The $99 bonus is in addition to the **<u>Bonus Chapter</u>** in this book titled **"Hot Internet tips and tools for exporters, importers."** Needless to say if you are a book-loving exporter or importer, you certainly need the Internet on your side as a powerful tool for finding genuine business partners and gaining much needed Internet exposure and publicity. That's why I want you to read "Hot Internet tips and tools for exporters, importers" which I included in **_Don't Africa Me_** as a special bonus for you.

Remember, all you have to do to get the $99 bonus is: simply forward the receipt you got when you bought **_Don't Africa Me_** to paashanbooks@mail.com, with "$99 Premium Book Writing Workshop Bonus" as subject line, and I will send you the premium workshop FREE of Charge.

So, what are you waiting for? Email me your receipt now and be on your way to becoming the powerful author of your dreams.

C. P. Eze, author **_Don't Africa Me_**

CONTENTS

vii

Foreword

The book you are holding in your hands creates better understanding among peoples of different nations, which is why I see it as being of utmost importance in today's world. I hope you will have the same level of enthusiasm to read it as I had reading it in Switzerland.

One thing that is often put on the back burner is the fact that every person on our mother earth is unique and has their vital role and contribution to the well being of the world community. That means when we accept everybody as we should, irrespective of their birth place, cultural background, religion or economic status, we take a great step forward towards peace on earth.

It was with great pleasure and deep understanding that I accepted the invitation from Paschal Eze to write the Foreword for his book, **_Don't Africa Me_**.

Having lived in the nineties in West African countries of The Gambia and Senegal, undertaking projects in Agriculture, Tourism, Fisheries and other fields, and offering start-up help as well for a nursery school with other friends, I readily recommend Paschal's book to everybody interested in Africa and its relevance and relationship to the rest of the world, knowing that this continent of 54 sovereign nations is more often than not misunderstood and its peoples stereotyped.

Remarkably, in today's media world, all peoples, including those in African countries like The Gambia and Senegal, have the opportunity to express their own opinions and share their wealth of information with others, and the best way to do this may well be the vast, underutilized possibilities of the Internet as this book clearly shows.

However, I must tell you that while implementing the aforementioned projects in The Gambia and neighboring Senegal, I witnessed a lot of corruption. But looking back at it now, I realize it was mostly perpetrated by foreign nations and companies, working with locals. The corruption in question opened my eyes and mind to the plight of African nations and their citizens.

I believe the various African nations must be allowed to direct their own socio-political and economic affairs, and learn from their own experiences on the path of development. Their leaders should be encouraged by what the Mo Ibrahim Foundation is doing to be more responsive to the needs and aspirations of their people.

Another touching part of Paschal's book is the issue of brain drain especially in the health sector. It is disturbing that well trained medical doctors and nurses leave countries like Zimbabwe, Nigeria and Ghana where they are greatly needed for the UK, Canada and United States, contributing to the further development of these wealthy nations.

While living in The Gambia, I visited a hospital with a fellow foreign expert and found 2-4 people sharing 1 bed, and this was during the malaria season. Some foreign doctors there showed me rooms filled with brand new, unused medical equipment laying there and gathering dust because of shortage of trained staff doctors and nurses.

My immediate reaction was to imagine the difference it could make if many African-born doctors and nurses in countries like United States of America, Canada and United Kingdom were to return to their home countries to help their own people and contribute more effectively to their countries' development.

African nations like Nigeria have many dynamic, intelligent and educated people in different parts of the world who need to contribute more effectively to the economic growth and development of their home countries and Paschal points their attention to trade and tourism as keys to development.

May be, African-born doctors can learn from the example of Swiss doctor Beat Richner's KANTHA BOPHA Children's Hospitals in Cambodia (www.beatocello.com) which are saving thousands of children's lives. At the invitation of the Cambodian government, Richner came to the country and renovated an old hospital and built new ones, with over 95% employees – nurses and doctors – being Cambodians.

In all, Paschal's book fantastically brings to the fore how ignorant and uninformed we sometimes are about Africa, and how we erroneously draw conclusions about the continent without getting the facts or even visiting it. Africa is a wonderful continent with tremendous heritage of authentic culture, natural medicine, wisdom and great respect and care for the elderly, among others. One wonders why it is not seen for its wonderful potentials and opportunities.

Africa is one of the richest if not the richest continent in the world for natural resources. Thus, when African nations properly utilize these resources and justly enjoy the profit from them through fair trade and responsible tourism, they will become prosperous, not overnight, but steadily. They will no longer

4

need charity donations. Instead, they will become donors in the long run!

This book is for me **THE** sign and hope that humanity can move a big step forward in accepting other peoples' uniqueness, learning from them, being tolerant and appreciating their vast potentials and cooperating with them in an open minded manner thus helping the world to become a better place.

So let's do it and not just talk about it. Let's act now!

My hope is that this book will be read by millions of people as it should. It is a fabulous, easily understandable work, with fully researched underlining information, making it useful and resourceful for book lovers in many nations - from students, politicians, investors, international traders and marketers to community activists, public servants, journalists and broadcasters.

I sincerely believe *Don't Africa Me* should be a must for business and international trade classes at universities and business schools around the world. It should be compulsory reading not only for US citizens and citizens of 54 African nations but also for other well meaning people around the world, as it would help them see peoples of Africa and their relevance and relationship to the rest of the world community in a deserving light.

Congratulations Paschal! Thank you for asking me to write this Foreword! God bless you and your family and all creation on mother earth.

May peace prevail on earth!

— Sesto Giovanni Castagnoli
Founder/President, World Spirit Forum, Zurich, Switzerland who lived and did business in African countries of The Gambia and Senegal in the 90s.

www.worldspiritforum.org/en

Introduction

Remember some decades ago when the "communist" China brand was anathema in America and many other industrialized nations?

I am glad you do because, as the US Chamber of Commerce explains in its September 2007 "Issues of Importance to American Business in the US-China Commercial Relationship" report, economic and trade issues were afterthoughts in discussions between US and China during President Nixon's groundbreaking China visit in 1972. The focus of the presidential visit had understandably been on diplomatic and security issues, not on trade because China wasn't yet a big player in trade.

Well, today, thirty five years later, most Americans now sleep in Chinese-made clothes on Chinese-made bedspreads under Chinese-made fans after watching sensational cable news on Chinese-made big screen TV sets and eating dinner made with Chinese-made spices and served with Chinese-made dish bowls or conveniently at nearby all-you-can-eat Chinese restaurants. Where is "communism" or rather the fear of it in all that? Nowhere!

Perhaps, it is only the peddle-fear-for-high-rating TV and radio commentators that still worry about "communist" China which has taken the world by storm with its multi-product diplomacy that has got many affordable products-loving Americans on its side, a multi-product diplomacy that warmly welcomed China into the lives of most Americans and, of course, Australians, Canadians, Nigerians and Namibians.

Instructively, China did not confine itself to the easy option of periodic defense of "communism" on American TV and in New York Times. Nor did it put all its diplomatic eggs in the visibly worn out basket of organizing expensive high-profile conferences and cocktail receptions that gave impatient attendees the opportunity to see its colorful flag and hear its lovely anthem. Such an approach would have failed woefully, leaving it to lick its psychological and economic wounds. It rather chose the strategic path of re-inventing and re-launching its image abroad not just in Washington DC and on Wall Street but more importantly on **Week Street**, which I see here as anywhere Americans live, work, pray or play.

> *"[China] rather chose the strategic path of re-inventing and re-launching its image abroad not just in Washington DC and on Wall Street but more importantly on Week Street, which I see here as anywhere Americans live, work, pray or play."*

The Chinese multi-consumer product diplomacy which I also call **lifestyle diplomacy** worked beyond measure to the common knowledge effect that China is now everywhere Americans look, and the fear of "communism" is practically gone, except on ultra protectionist TV and radio shows whose hosts, I must say, are exercising their well deserved free speech rights.

In case you are wondering why "communism" is in quotes, the fact is that contrary to widely held opinion even on highly rated TV programs, there has never been and there will never be a communist country. Communism is a quintessential utopia while socialism, the quaky waiting room for the emergence of communist euphoria, has at best been a supine reality as I discussed in permissible detail in Chapter Seven of this book.

Note however that I am not defending or promoting China whose human rights record and support for the genocidal regime in Khartoum I detest and openly condemn. But I must state that I admire China's strategic international marketing and brand management skills and resolve. That is why in *Don't Africa Me*, I show why and how African countries like Nigeria and Kenya could methodically win the geo-branding war on them with strategic image replacement and re-branding, following the example of China which successfully replaced its dreaded image as a "communist" nation with a good image among the poor and middle class majority as the biggest source of affordable goods from toys to clothes.

Remember the bad image of Vietnam during and many years after the Vietnam War? Well, Vietnam was on October 16, 2007 unanimously elected into the UN Security Council for a two-year term, in evidence of its diplomatic resurgence. Here is how President Nguyen Minh Triet of Vietnam described current US-Vietnam relations in his June 22, 2007 visit to the White House: "It's very impressive that yesterday I had a chance to visit a farmer who raised grapes. And the life is very happy, and **they have a warmth of feelings toward Vietnam**. And the owner had to hug me several times, hesitating to say good-bye to us. And that demonstrates the desire for friendship between our two peoples." Put differently, the Vietnamese government believes in **front porch diplomacy** which is yielding desired positive results in the US, unlike Nigeria that seemingly treats its blend of photo-op diplomacy and black-tie dinner diplomacy in Washington DC as sacred while many people across the US retain their negative view of Nigeria as a no-go area.

> *"Vietnamese government believes in front porch diplomacy which is yielding desired positive results in the US, unlike Nigeria that seemingly treats its blend of photo-op diplomacy and black-tie dinner diplomacy in Washington DC as sacred while many people across the US retain their negative view of Nigeria as a no-go area."*

For his part, Triet's host, President George W. Bush, stated: "I explained to the President we want to have good relations with Vietnam. And **we've got good economic relations**. We signed a Trade and Investment Framework Agreement. And I was impressed by the growing Vietnamese economy."

That's true. Vietnam reportedly had a GDP growth of 8.17% in 2006, and is part of Goldman Sachs

Next 11 (N-11) economies with good investmentand future growth prospects, alongside **Nigeria**, South Korea, Egypt, Indonesia, Bangladesh, Iran, Mexico, Philippines, Pakistan and Turkey.

The US is now one of Vietnam's biggest trading partners, and according to Raymond F. Burghardt, former US ambassador to that country, in a September 24, 2003 speech at the annual meeting of the American Chamber of Commerce in Hanoi, "until less than 10 years ago Vietnam was a very isolated country." Remarkably, Vietnam did not remain isolated and its image did not remain bad, which is instructive to African nations like Nigeria that are still under the spell of the crowded Brand Africa closet that is denigrated by main street or the Northern corporate media-trumpeted misdeeds of a very tiny segment of their populations.

Don't Africa Me is therefore not an exercise in repudiating the African continent of my extraction or dishonoring its over 740 million inhabitants and the over 100 million "Africans" in the Diaspora who share that honor and heritage with me. It is rather a bold-faced reality check aimed at refocusing and repositioning sovereign African nations like Nigeria, Botswana, Mauritius, Kenya and South Africa in the target market of America, away from the limiting, nay, suffocating Brand Africa closet of American refrain and following compelling strategic marketing and re-branding examples of the Asian nations of China, Japan and Vietnam.

> *"They lack popular and wide appeal mainly because of continuous corporate media pounding, poor investment in strategic marketing, less than impressive political will and monumentally rigid preference for Washington DC photo-op and black-tie dinner diplomacy."*

If the level of stand-alone appeal, the volume and steady flow of foreign direct investments, the volume of product and service exports, the number of tourist inflows and the effectiveness of **lifestyle diplomacy** in target markets as compared to other countries are good yardsticks for measuring the success of nation brands, the aforementioned African nations would not be seen as successful nation brands. They lack popular and wide appeal mainly because of continuous corporate media pounding, poor investment in strategic marketing, less than impressive political will and monumentally rigid prefer-ence for Washington DC photo-op and black-tie dinner diplomacy.

That's why, while I understand and appreciate the sentiment behind the preference of many of **my sub-Saharan African-born interviewees to be called Africans, as you will read in Chapter Two,** I believe it is basically unfair to call me an African, instead of a Nigerian (or New Nigerian), and then turn around and call someone from America an American, instead of a North American. But that's what many people do. They fail to see the individual existence of Nigeria (and therefore Nigerians), for instance, and instead refer to Africa (and Africans) even though Africa is a continent of 54 countries.

This, in my view, greatly affects trade and tourism on the continent, thus making re-branding a blazing ne-cessity. But here is how I differ from many people on the issue. They crave for a comprehensive re-branding of the continent, which is understandable. I believe any effort at re-branding Africa as a whole, instead of its cities like Johannesburg, and sovereign countries like Nigeria, is counterproductive. The rea-son is simply that most people in target markets like America, Canada, Britain and China clearly think more in terms of cities and nations than of conti-nents.

They respond more favorably to an October 02-11, 2007 Special Olympics in Shanghai and an August 08-24, 2008 Olympics in Beijing than a July 2009 'Dream Sports Festival' or 'Wholesale Trade Fair' in Asia. They appreciate the United Arab Emirates city of Dubai as home of the world's tallest and only 7-star hotel, the 1060 feet high and sail-shaped Burj al-Arab (meaning Tower of the Arabs), even as the city is now pushing itself as a major global financial hub, and attracting huge investments from around the world. Yes, **Americans recognize and appreciate countries and cities that are set apart, not the ones in the crowded Brand Africa closet.**

And tourism and trade have an awful lot more to do with cities as Cancun in Mexico and nations like China in Asia and their distinguishable products and services than lumping them together as they do with the continent of Africa. The more members of the corporate media and their geo-branding allies on Main Street and Wall Street lump African countries together, the more they undermine or suppress the visibility, uniqueness and competitiveness of these countries, which is unfair.

> *"The various chapters of Don't Africa Me paint an insider's picture of a continent that is certainly not mendicant of hope and means but of well-thought-out and sustained people-focused developmental actions that draw extensively from an understanding of global socio-economic realities and dynamics."*

However, expressing such a blunt and realistic view is not to suggest Africa is in such a sorry irredeemable state that beckons nothing but passivity and safe distance from its peoples. Far from it! The various chapters of *Don't Africa Me* paint an insider's picture of a continent that is certainly not mendicant of hope and means but of well-thought-out and sustained people-focused developmental actions that draw extensively from an understanding of global socio-economic realities and dynamics.

As you will discover through the pages of *Don't Africa Me*, I am not in the comity of thousands of professionals from African countries like Nigeria who, upon their effort-intensive, appreciable wage-

16

centric integration into countries like America, shy away from their **coffee table diplomacy** role, walking instead on the non-strategic path of attending African potlucks, visiting and sending money infrequently to adulating relatives back home and building big vacation homes there to defend their trophy-like Diaspora ego.

Don't get me wrong. I commend those who help few relatives back home, as I do, and organize African potlucks, as I don't. I believe Africa's problem is not solvable through feel-good ethnic events in Detroit or Des Moines, dispensation of handouts from Juffureh to Jos and ego trips in Accra or Abuja. Nor could it be solved through marketing-challenged armchair diplomacy in Washington and London in a world where the branding savvy gets it all.

I remain enamored of my birth (of English-speaking and God-fearing parents) amid jubilations from extended family of farmers and city dwellers, fully breastfed without crowd-pleasing recourse to the modern god of convenience, and rigorously bred and educated under the tourist enchanting but northern media stigmatized Nigerian sun. I have lived in or traveled extensively in a number of African countries like Republic of The Gambia, Ghana, Senegal and Ivory Coast and I greatly value my memorable hands-on experiences there. **I not only dined and dialogued with the elite but I also** mingled and munched with the ordinary people to see life through their own lenses.

The point I am making here is that many in the north who claim to be Africa experts do so in keeping with the "better-than-thou" tradition and on the insidious "dark continent" premise. Many lay claim to expertise on Africa just because (a) they made a couple of "feel good" official or private visits to Nairobi or Monrovia, (b) they listened to bamboozling lectures by those who merely attended some cultural festivals in Gambia, (c) they read history books written by those who attended Ghana's independence ceremony in 1957 and have since then lost touch with a continent whose constituent nations have undergone socio-political and especially economic changes, (d) they attended a black-tie dinner held in Washington DC by Nigeria or (e) they have followed news reports on TV without exercising the ability to separate the wheat from the chaff, and to dig deeper for truth about the African continent that has been besieged by global misinformation and at times outright ignorance of its realities, strengths and challenges.

So, I know Africa's problem is not the non-Hollywood-like living conditions of many of its peoples as some people hold true. I have seen poverty, instability, disease, illiteracy and corruption (the PI-DIC syndrome explained in Chapter One) outside Africa. I have seen real poverty amid real plenty in cities like London, Detroit and Chicago, and I have heard well rehearsed "same ol,' same ol' " political circumlocution on them.

My conclusion therefore is that Africa's problem is simply and squarely a branding problem. There has been a branding war on the image-vulnerable tourism and trade sectors of African countries like Nigeria, Kenya, Zimbabwe and Uganda which hold the key to their sustained development. As advanced as the common stock of humanity has become, **there is still a prevailing perception in many industrialized countries that Africa is a place half-naked people run around with hunting spears – just because of the unrelenting Afriscare (my portmanteau for media propelled scare about Africa) thrust on television, movies and public events.** Such a funny, quarter-mile perception, as you can readily imagine, magnetizes the hasty conclusion that "Africa" is incapable of producing quality goods and services or being a safe and enjoyable tourist destination.

Unfortunately, this blatant branding problem is not being properly tackled at the moment by African countries who are engaged in collective sporadic and reactionary continent re-branding efforts which I hold futile.

> *"Africa's problem is simply and squarely a branding problem. There has been a branding war on the image-vulnerable tourism and trade sectors of African countries..."*

That is why the loud-screaming challenge even the deaf could hear is for well articulated and sustained city and nation re-branding from Jos to Johannesburg and Nigeria to Namibia. This is more so when African leaders are now trumpeting Africa's need for more trade, and not more aid. They are right! Feed the Children's late night ads on TV -parading hunger-stricken children - will, no doubt, attract donations from compassionate Americans but certainly not trade and tourism with African countries. AGOA or no AGOA, African countries like Gambia or Ghana do not come to mind when Americans think of importing consumer products.

And that's a theme that runs through the whole *Don't Africa Me* book. Trade and tourism have a lot to do with image, and that of African countries like Zimbabwe and Nigeria is as pummeled today as "communist" China's decades ago. China wisely re-branded itself and won the hearts and minds of most American consumers, despite recent widespread concerns over health risks associated with lead found in Chinese toys. US-based Mattel, the world's number 1 toy company, even had to apologize to China for embarrassment caused by the resultant toy recalls, blaming itself for design flaws that primarily caused the problem. Believe me, that couldn't have happened in 1972 when China was not the inescapable trade powerhouse it has now become. Could Mattel have apologized to Nigeria if the products in question were from Nigeria? I doubt it.

It is therefore time for Brand Africa to be dismantled, and in its place the reinvented, reinvigorated, refocused and repositioned Brand Nigeria, Brand South Africa, Brand Ghana or Brand Kenya that can attract more meaningful and sustainable trade and tourism and significantly boost their development.

That's what ***Don't Africa Me*** is all about, and you can be sure it is not a harvest of jargons but of the sometimes scarce common sense.

So, read and let others read too!
C. Paschal Eze, CEC
Re-branding strategist and certified e-commerce consultant
Email: paschal(no spam)paschalezemedia.com

Don't Africa Me

Chapter One

The PIDIC Syndrome

I believe there will always be image Darwinism and brand Darwinism which ride exclusively on advantage and strength. There will always be individuals, organizations and nations that glare on the pedestal of their intelligently engineered brand equity and those that live or are made to live under the heavy weight of such pedestal.

That's why - in today's world of slim-fit fascination - Americans hear little or nothing of the seemingly efficacious weight loss pill Hoodia made of South African desert plant Hoodia gordonii. Blame it on the Brand Africa construct of "we are terrific, you are terrible" refrain, and you are right but politically incorrect.

TV news images Americans see of Kenya and Nigeria are about refuse heaps in slums and alarming despair while those they see of China and Vietnam are of manufacturing plants and modern infrastructure. These carefully shot and projected TV images clearly shape perceptions and attitudes of Americans towards other countries just as global giant CNN and globally marketed and sold Hollywood movies shape perceptions and attitudes of other peoples - especially developing countries like South Africa, Kenya and Nigeria - towards America and Americans.

Do South Africa, Kenya and Nigeria have fully functioning manufacturing plants and modern infrastructure? They do. Is Vietnam better developed and more democratic than Nigeria? No! According to Obiageli Katryn Ezekwesili, the Nigerian-born World Bank's Vice President for Africa, **"in countries such as Kenya and Senegal, firms are as competitive as those in fast-growing Asian economies such as India and Vietnam." (1)** The difference may well be that Nigeria is in Brand Africa seen through the lens of destitution and despair and Vietnam is visible as Brand Vietnam seen through the lens of near ubiquitous boldly signposted Vietnamese restaurants, among other things.

Yet, Nigeria is the fifth largest oil supplier to the US - behind Canada, Mexico, Saudi Arabia and Venezuela – and TV images of American Chevron's oil drilling operations in Nigeria are quintessential rarities just as big Made-in-Nigeria signposts at gas stations are stupendously utopian.

Chapter One: The PIDIC Syndrome

Despite the spectacular catchphrase that the world is a global village, which supposes a plethora of geo-cultural extroverts, a dispensation of infectious cultural openness and respect for our shared humanity, many people I have encountered from America and Canada to Australia have shown a mind-boggling denigration of Africa.

Though a New York-based emerging markets investment bank that invested $161 million in a Nigerian bank in May 2007 sees such investment as indicative of their "high degree of confidence ... in the bank and in the economy of Nigeria," **(2)** there are still Americans who see Nigeria as a cluster of huts in the lion-filled Africa jungle in keeping with the **Afriscare** (my portmanteau for media propelled scare about Africa) thrust of television and movie images.

And while Nigeria is said to be the third fastest growing GSM market in the world, and I could make a 24-7 call from Iowa City or Detroit to a rural dwelling peasant farmer in Nigeria and speak with her on her ever present imported cell phone made with coltan from Democratic Republic of Congo, there are still Americans who ask me if women there could say their names, if children have real toys, if men are only hunters, peasant farmers and idol worshippers, if people make human sacrifices to gods and if lions roam around like Coralville rabbits. They

25

ask me if my "hut" in Nigeria is in close proximity to that of someone from a far African country like Kenya, Ethiopia, Seychelles, Mauritius or Botswana. They ask me if people in Africa run around half-naked with spears.

> *"They ask me whether people in Africa run around half-naked with spears."*

That's the 21st Century Africa of their imagination, one that radically differs from the African continent I know, study and analyze. Theirs is an Africa that, consequent upon the selectively chosen and projected images and views on their TV sets, is radically bereft of good things, comfort, wealthy people, civility, security and modernity. Theirs is an Africa that has nothing to do with meaningful trade and tourism even though, unbeknown to them, the African country of Nigeria has one of the world's highest gas reserves, and a vibrant Nigerian Stock Exchange with capitalization projected to reach $100 billion by end of 2008. Nigerian banks are listed on the London Stock Exchange. Many Nigerian banks appeared on The Banker Magazine's 2006 Top 1000 banks of the world while that of 2007 ranked Nigeria's Intercontinental Bank Plc as the second fastest growing bank in the world. **(3)** "Goldman Sachs also predicts that Nigeria will be the 12th largest economy in the world ahead of Italy, Canada and others." **(4)**

Yet, many people in America quickly race down the PIDIC path when Africa is mentioned or someone is called an African. They think only of five things that often evoke pity or prejudice, namely:

P – Poverty

I – Instability

D- Disease

I - Illiteracy

C - Corruption

There is no gainsaying the fact that Nigeria, for instance, has been corruption-ridden since its independence from Britain in 1960. As Nuhu Ribadu, chairman of Nigeria's Economic and Financial Crimes Commission (EFCC), told the BBC in October 2006, over $380 billion was stolen or wasted by Nigerian governments from independence in 1960 to the end of military rule in 1999. **(5)** Human Rights Watch estimated that between $4 and $8 billion was stolen each year from 1999 to 2007 during the Obasanjo civilian administration. **(6)** Imagine what those stolen monies could have done for ordinary

27

hardworking Nigerians who have been repeatedly abused by their self-serving "leaders." But I am happy that, at least, the EFCC had reportedly recovered $5 billion as at the time of the news report.

Zaire, now Democratic Republic of Congo, still suffers from the cancer of Mobutu Sese Seko's kleptocracy. Mobutu, its former ruler, reportedly stole over $5 billion and led very extravagant lifestyle while his people languished. You may not find up to 10 past and present "leaders" in Africa who have not exercised devastating diligence in defrauding women and children, the disabled and the elderly.

> *"You may not find up to 10 past and present "leaders" in Africa who have not exercised devastating diligence in defrauding women and children, the disabled and the elderly."*

But my point is that corruption is not unique to Nigeria or any other African country.

A 2007 report by the US-based Carnegie Endowment for International Peace says the Chinese economy loses $86bn (£42bn) a year to corruption. "Even after adjusting for inflation, the sums of money looted by government officials today are astonishing," the report said, adding, however, that the Chinese government has been tackling the problem. **(7)**

Iraq, for instance, is a violently corrupt country. Here is what Judge Radhi Hamza al-Radhi, former commissioner of the Iraqi Commission on Public Integrity, told a House Panel in October 2007: "They are so corrupt that they will attack their accusers and their families with guns and meat hooks, as well as countercharges of corruption." **(8)** Other countries around the world have their own portions and patterns of corruption, but that does not diminish the fact that it is bad.

No doubt Nigeria's roads are poorly maintained, its railway system collapsed decades ago, the waterways are grossly underutilized and domestic flights are expensive, thus putting heavy pressure on the roads which are flooded with more affordable imported "second-hand" cars especially popular brands like Toyota Camry and Honda Accord. Others see this as a big problem that provokes hopelessness but I see it as a beckoning challenge, a huge opportunity for savvy domestic and foreign investors and for better people-focused leadership. I know this because I rode on both the good and the screaming-to-be repaired Nigerian roads in April 2007.

However, I have also been on some poor roads in America though I must admit they are better maintained than many Nigerian roods. Remember the August 1, 2007 evening rush hour collapse into the Mississippi River of the I-35W bridge in Minneapolis? That was a major incident underscoring poor maintenance of America's infrastructure. Barely two weeks later, on August 14, a 140-foot-high bridge under construction in China's tourist city of Fenghuang collapsed leaving about 36 people dead. The British Broadcasting Corporation (BBC) reported that "China has identified more than 6,000 bridges that are damaged or dangerous." **(9)**

While I sympathize with families who lost their loved ones in these two unfortunate incidents in America and China, the point remains that poor infrastructure is not the exclusive preserve of African countries and should therefore not be religiously cited by individuals as excuse for shunning such countries' trade and tourism. Every country has its own share of people who do poor jobs, and I dislike poor jobs.

Yet, the corporate media persistently hollers into the sub-consciousness of its captive audiences that the African continent is squarely synonymous with PIDIC, thus promoting ignorance about the real Africa of visible challenges and little known opportunities.

Disturbing self-inflicted wounds

But it would be wrong for me to suggest the American corporate media is alone in this unrelenting image onslaught. Many immigrant parents from African countries like Nigeria, DRC, Ghana and Kenya are fond of telling their children "If you do that again, I will send you to Africa" as if the African continent were a very lonely prison cell or petrifying torture chamber. So, their lovely children grow up with very wrong impression of Africa, associating it with the worst form of human existence. The change of Africa's battered image abroad should, no doubt, begin with such parents and their offspring.

> *"Immigrant parents from African countries are fond of telling their children "If you do that again, I will send you to Africa" as if the African continent was a very lonely prison cell or petrifying torture chamber. So, their children grow up with very wrong impression of Africa, associating it with the worst form of human existence."*

In 2006, the African American Museum in Cedar

31

Rapids Iowa invited me to present my "Turn off your TV and see Africa" seminar to a largely White audience. I presented a SWOT analysis of African countries like Nigeria, Ghana and Botswana. Then came time for questions, which is my best part. Guess who quickly stood up to say in a nutshell that Africa was up to no good. A Nigerian-born Roman Catholic reverend sister living in Iowa. She was part of a charity that provided aid to some Nigerian schools, and had apparently come to the well promoted event to canvass for donations. She rambled about how **all** Nigerian roads were **very bad**, how the Ikeja Lagos airport was **terrible**, and so on, with her White colleague echoing that she never saw anybody in Nigeria who wasn't poor.

The fact is: Everyone in Nigeria isn't poor but everyone in Nigeria isn't rich. Nigeria not only has its share of poor people but also an educated and comfortable middle class and an undoubtedly rich upper class. Even America, the richest nation on earth, has visibly poor people from New Orleans and Washington DC to Detroit and Chicago. There are many bad roads in Nigeria but there are good roads as well. Besides, the Lagos-situated Murtala Mohammed International Airport of today is comparable to many airports around the world, following substantial improvements since 2000. This busy airport was patterned after Amsterdam's Schiphol Airport in the Netherlands. But Nigeria has other major airports, including the Nnamdi Azikiwe International Airport in its capital, Abuja.

Alas, the pity-evoking Nigeria of the donation-seeking sister was different from my own Nigeria of realities and opportunities. I was baffled, to say the least, that she could propel the PIDIC image in such a way, just to get donations for her school projects in Nigeria. Such unfortunate actions greatly hurt African countries especially when it comes to trade and tourism

Revealing facts and figures

Though about 14% of the world's population live on the African continent, Africa's international tourist arrivals account for only 4% of the world total, according to figures from the World Tourism Organization. Note, however, that despite its much publicized political crisis, sit-tight President Robert Mugabe's Zimbabwe in September 2007 announced 24% increase in tourist arrivals, with Caribbean Islands and Asian countries as major source markets.**(10)**

Wondering what then is my problem since Zimbabwe is having increased tourist arrivals? Read this: The Zimbabwean Tourism Authority chief executive, Karikoga Kaseke, was quoted as saying the growth in the Caribbean market was not only because of increased marketing activities in the region but mainly because "That market has not been **polluted** by the bad publicity that we have experienced in the West, especially the UK." **(11)**

> *"Though about 14% of the world's population live on the African continent, its international tourist arrivals account for only 4% of the world total, according to figures from the World Tourism Organization."*

Kaseke went on to lament, "But Europe, especially the UK, has been affected by the bad publicity and that market has remained a problem child. The UK is the nerve centre of the negative publicity because their propaganda machinery is far more resourced than ours. Last week, there was a damaging documentary on the BBC." **(12)**

Before I proceed, let me state unequivocally that while I like the lovely country of Zimbabwe and its people, it is not my intention to defend it here. This is more so because I personally dislike sit-tight leaders and dynasties, north or south. Ten years are certainly more than enough for any politician anywhere to effect any positive, people-benefiting change they ever sincerely planned and resolved to implement. And nobody can be the be-it-all of stability, growth and development in any human society. Each person should do their best and honorably leave the stage for others to do theirs too.

That noted, can you believe that the so called "propaganda" against Zimbabwe did not stop the UK from "siphoning" Zimbabwean nurses? While the country's health care system was reportedly "close to collapse," the UK was further draining its healthcare manpower, hiring 1,610 of its estimated 9000 nurses. "One fifth of Zimbabwe's trained nurses were recruited to work in Britain last year - despite rules supposedly banning hospitals from poaching staff from the world's poorest countries." **(13)** Do you get my point?

On international trade, the British Broadcasting Corporation (BBC) reported in 2004 that exports from African countries decreased from 6.3% of the world total in 1980 to 2.5% in 2004. **(14)** According to the World Bank, "over the past three decades, Africa has become ever more marginalized from trade at the global level. Africa's share of world exports has dropped by nearly 60 percent, a staggering loss of $70 billion annually, equivalent to 21 percent of the region's GDP and more than five times the $13 billion in annual aid flows to Africa." **(15)** Isn't that alarming? While Africa's share of world trade was falling, that of the Asian country of China was increasing tremendously. **(16)**

> *"Experts say a 1% increase in Africa's minute share of world trade would fetch it $70 billion annually, which is significantly higher and better than all the aid and debt relief it receives."*

Experts say a 1% increase in Africa's minute share of world trade would fetch it $70 billion annually, which is significantly higher and better than all the aid and debt relief it receives. Thus, trade is key to Africa's future, the same trade the well promoted PIDIC image undermines.

The African continent comprising 54 countries is very far behind in the area of international trade in services. As one source put it, "Trade in services is the fastest growing area in international trade, amounting to $1,350 billion in 1999, about a quarter of the figure for trade in goods. But Africa's share of this is small -- about 2 per cent annually." **(17)** And I blame it largely on Brand Africa that is viewed through the PIDIC lens.

The African Growth and Opportunity Act (AGOA) said to be aimed at facilitating duty-free US imports from 48 sub-Saharan African countries has not really delivered the goods for the same reason. American businesses and consumers don't think of sub-Saharan African countries when it comes to importing or buying consumer products. They very unfortunately think of PIDIC, which I explained above. But why shouldn't they when they are **Afriscared** (my portmanteau for being scared about Africa) by carefully shot and constantly shown TV images of "African" AIDS patients and orphans, scavengers and child soldiers versus footages of Chinese and Indian factories, finished products, seaports and good roads? Why shouldn't they when many African nations do little or nothing about it, apparently waiting for the well coordinated image bombardment to cease?

Where are trade and tourism promotion in all those footages that have served to evoke pity or fear, reinforcing the PIDIC image? They simply make African countries like Kenya, Republic of The Gambia and Liberia more attractive to fundraising and aid-giving NGOS than American importers, exporters, investors and tourists that will help in stimulating economic growth in those countries. They guarantee that the Pity Africa "Industry" remains a multi billion dollar one marketing despair with ravaging intensity.

> *"They guarantee that the Pity Africa "Industry" remains a multi billion dollar one marketing despair with ravaging intensity."*

Don't get me wrong. I love America and Americans just as I love Britain and Britons but I believe it is fashionable in America and Britain, among other industrialized countries, to say or do things that keep many unique and attractive things that run from Nigeria to Namibia in despicable oblivion – far removed from public glare and knowledge – to ensure these sub-Saharan African countries remain dependable sources of raw materials and cheap labor, not of competing finished products.

So, in case you think there aren't quality finished products in African countries, I readily suggest you visit these sites on seven of Africa's 54 countries and see for yourself. I chose only seven countries because I don't want to overlabor you.

Nigeria: http://www.nigeriaexport.com/products, http://www.nepcng.com

South Africa: http://www.southafrica.info/, http://www.wosa.co.za/, http://www.webtraders.co.za/

Kenya: http://epckenya.org/cbik/index.asp

Ghana:
http://www.gepcghana.com/ghexporters.php

Botswana:
http://www.exporters.bw/members.htm

Mauritius: http://www.makeitmauritius.com

Egypt: www.export-egypt.com

But don't just stop there. Do a Google search for their commercial attaches at their various embassies in Washington DC, Ottawa or London and see if they can be of some help to you. Unfortunately, many of them aren't as proactive, energetic and dynamic as they should be in promoting their countries' export products. They wait for positive things to happen instead of making positive things happen, which is why they should learn from their counterparts from India, Singapore, Malaysia, South Korea,

Vietnam, Japan and especially China who do awesome jobs.

Chapter Two

Do continental sentiments make cents?

I do not mince words about it. Though advance fee fraud perpetrated by an absolute minority of Nigerians at home has earned Nigeria a bad image in many countries from America to Australia and even the most morally-geared Nigerian professionals and achievers in those countries are needlessly seen as guilty until proven innocent by twist of fate, I prefer to be called a Nigerian (or a New Nigerian), not an African.

Such bold preference is not oblivious of the fact that naming has a lot to do with branding, and nation rebranding has a lot to do with identity and image. But:

A. Calling me an African is fundamentally devoid of fairness because people from other continents are identified by their national identities, not their continental identities. Canadians and Americans are not called North Americans but Canadians and Americans. Nor are the British and French called Europeans but British and French. Why should mine be different? Africa is not Australia which is both a continent and a country.

B. Calling me an African means lumping together 54 countries under a continental identity that perpetuates the mainstream media-driven PIDIC Syndrome – in which Africa is viewed only through the scare-drenched lens of Poverty, Instability, Disease, Illiteracy and Corruption. This is in practical terms condescending to me and unhelpful to Nigeria which has its own image problems.

C. Calling Nobel Peace Prize winner and former UN secretary general, Kofi Annan, an African robs his country, Ghana, of the opportunity to benefit from his great achievements as it competes in the global marketplace. This is more so when media attention on him could lead more curious and beyond-the-surface-scratch reporters into his birth city of Kumasi to directly or indirectly highlight its friendly educated people, little known tourist attractions, export products and investment opportunities. The same is true of international statesman and Nobel

Peace Prize winner, Nelson Mandela of South Africa, first environmentalist winner of Nobel Peace Prize and founder of the Green Belt Movement, Dr. Wangari Maathai of Kenya, and Nobel Literature Laureate Wole Soyinka of Nigeria. After all, big names drive a lot of things like tourism marketing, trade promotion, event promotion and movie sales in our big name-obsessed world.

D. Calling me an African does not challenge geographical and touristo-trade curiosity in the Northern Hemisphere especially since many intellectuals of diverse races are now saying all life emanated from Africa. In other words, they are saying Africa belongs to everyone on the face of the earth, and not just to citizens of African countries.

Many disagree with me but it's their right

On whether people of African origin should be called and addressed by their national identities or their collective continental identity, I am very happily in the minority as the comments you will read below clearly show. The differing views and preferences are indeed healthy. I believe efficacious ideas are often offshoots of dialectics of thought, which is why I emailed professionals of African origin in different parts of the world, asking them to tell me if they preferred to be called Africans or Nigerians, Gambians, Kenyans, Ethiopians, Senegalese, Ghanaians, as the case may be. I also asked a Jamaican-born author in America to weigh in on the issue.

Here are the responses I got:

"Honestly, I increasingly find myself identifying with being an African than Nigerian. This is because of my training and education. I believe that I have read very wide and seem to see the problems of the African within a continental context. Nigeria is just a part of the African problem.

Moreover, there is the racial dimension to our problems which I find many who lead Africa are woefully ignorant of. Many people do not seem to understand how Africa has been greatly impacted by our colonial past and relations with the non-African world. Because of this ignorance, the so-called leaders of Africa today are very myopic and fail to adequately address international and global issues as these affect them.

Of course, I will readily admit that the exposure that I have had, by residing in the West for 27 years, has affected my worldview and perspectives. But I seem to see that my internationalism is better furthered by my identification with the Africanness which I hold dearly rather than by my Nigerianness. Nigeria's matters will be easily resolved when we have a

Chapter Two: Do continental sentiments make cents?

truly visionary leader who can understand the matters that affect the Africans most."

— E.S. Etuk, Ph.D, award-winning author, speaker, and professional historian who has been heard on more than 200 radio talk-shows and television programs in USA, Canada, the Caribbean and Europe.

"I prefer, without doubt, to be called an African for I, a Blackman, was born an African before there was any such thing as Gambia or Gambian. An 'African' is what genuinely characterizes me as a Blackman for that is why every member of the Black race in every part of the world is defined by his/her African heritage, whether he/she appreciates Africa or not; Blacks born and bred in America are referred to as African-Americans, those in the UK as African British/Brits while those in the Caribbean are called Afro/African-Caribbeans.

Africa is the positively complex continent the rest of the world continues to despise, but that rest of the world can't do without. Africa is the exceptional continent with rich cultures and cultural values, and a land of self esteem and prestige, despite the lack of enough bread for everyone.

It is only being African that associate me with celebrated global icons such as Mandela, Sisulu, Tutu, Annan, Sankara, Nkrumah, Kenyatta, Lumumba, Biko, among many.

So I am proud to be referred to as an African and nothing else."

— **Sheriff Bojang Jr., Gambian-born journalist in Senegal**

"*I think I would prefer to be called an African. The reason is that outside the African continent every black man is identified with Africa, and we see ourselves as one regardless of the nationality. The burden of developing Africa is one that we need to confront as a single entity (regardless of our nationality) to be able to develop a synergy in utilizing the enormous human and material resources that are available in Africa to transform the continent to achieve the greatness that it was created to achieve. If the continent of Europe with the level of development are actively working towards unity to be able to take full advantage of the opportunities that globalization has offered, then Africa needs it more, in order not to be the "dustbin" of the rest of the world.*
I have nothing against being called a Nigerian, but that will belittle the challenge ahead of me. So, I prefer tackling it head-long, instead of playing the ostrich."

— **Ngozi Abiodun Nwogwugwu, MPA, Human Capital Development & Investment Consultant.**
ngozinwogwuwgwu@aol.com;
ngozi@kuneassociates.com, Nigeria

Chapter Two: Do continental sentiments make cents?

"I guess I prefer being called an African. It's mainly because I do not see any differences between myself and a Senegalese woman bar the (foreign) language difference. Also, on my travels across the continent, I've come to realize that being Nigerian, Gambian or Senegalese is just a mindset. The things we have in common far outweigh our differences..."

— Ndey Tapha Sosseh, MA, Partner/Administrator, Association of Development Consultants (ADCO), Republic of The Gambia

"Nigerian!"

— Bola Oginni, MA, President, Miss Hotlegs Nigeria, Event director, Finishing Touch Events, United Kingdom

"Unless you are from Jamaica or the Bahamas, I assume you are African. However, most Americans don't know a lot about Africa's geography, so they might not know where a country is, and could ask if it is in Africa."

— Aimee McDonald, Certified Nursing Assistant, USA

"I see Nigeria (and any other African nation) as a component of Africa. So, I am first an African (and proudly so) and then a Nigerian (proudly so too). Unfortunately, because many Africans are very ethnic (or tribalistic as they say), they

47

identify only with their country (and even more so their village and ethnic make-up) and superficially with Africa as a whole.

The fact that I see myself first as an African and then a Nigerian does not mean that my allegiance to Nigeria is any less than any other citizen. It simply means that I have decided not to contribute to the enormous divisions that already exist among and between African nations and their citizens, when we all should really see ourselves as part of a whole (Africa).

So, in a nutshell, I will like to be identified both as a Nigerian and an African."

— Dr. Jacyee Aniagolu, Pharmaceutical Research Scientist, Writer and Author, USA

"For me, Africa comes first. Therefore, I prefer to be called an African instead of a Gambian, although I am a holder of a Gambian passport. I would have preferred to travel with an Africa Union passport.

I believe that for us to quickly turn the African unity dream into reality, we must first deal with the identity issue. By identifying ourselves as African citizens, we will be able to diffuse the continent's many day-to-day challenging colonial differences or divides. With the achievement of a continental unity, Africa will fit well in the new global economy, create a common market and common currency as well as stimulate economic development.

48

Chapter Two: Do continental sentiments make cents?

Due to colonialism, citizens of countries with similar tribes and sharing boundaries tend to see each other as enemies instead of brothers committed to pursuing a common interest or promoting the spirit of African unity...

As an African journalist, I always feel comfortable with identifying myself as an African."

— Musa Saidykhan, Gambian journalist based in Senegal

"I would love to be called a Nigerian, not an African. I have met many people who thought I was sharing my habitation in Africa with wild animals like snakes and lions just because I had told them I was from Africa. Though I did not like their notion of Africa, I welcomed their openness. It was apparent the mass media had brainwashed them into believing Africa was very primitive. On the other hand, Nigeria is a country divinely blessed with abundant natural resources and high level manpower that when effectively harnessed by conscientious leaders would make it the true giant of Africa and the entire Black world. So, while I love Africa, I prefer to be called a Nigerian."

— Frank Dara, Revival Day Ministries, author
Troubled? Fill your life with joy and power

"Depending on whom you are talking with and where you want your thesis to lead, I am African and Nigerian. This is analyzing the racial equation as purely a function of access.

I will certainly sound more reasonable if I put my pies in one plate and decide to choose. Then I am African first, foremost and more meaningfully. There are huge insights today as to the exponential costs — hidden or obvious — of being Nigerian in the Diaspora.

For the same reasons I am Nigerian, I can be African because with both identities I can graciously extol the cultural, religious, historical, and linguistic diversities of my world. So, coming from Nigeria and being part of the glory that came together with other countries of the most misunderstood continent, I say that I am an African.

My position detaches me from making any moral judgments on our collective past; it helps me not to dwell on the history of slavery and a succession of European colonizers. It makes me stronger because in living my Bantu identity, I will always want to greet you: Sawu Bona hoping that I will hear you say: Sikhona.

I am AFRICAN!"

— **Osita Aniemeka, USA**

"The identity preference is dependent on the audience. For Americans, it is better to be referred to as an African (a

Chapter Two: Do continental sentiments make cents?

synonym for "Black") for there is a significant ignorance on African geography especially among younger Americans.

I would rather be referred to as an African than someone asking me how big my city is, referring to Kenya, or someone thinking I'm from the Arab world "north of Saudi Arabia".

However, when among Africans, I prefer to wear my Kenyan identity for then, I have the confidence that the person understands me better if they know the country I'm from. If only there were a better geographical understanding, then I would rather be succinct and
identify myself as a Kenyan."

— Martin Nwangi, USA

"Nigerian."

— Dr. Edward Nwanegbo, research physician who was among the University of Pittsburg researchers who discovered the SARS corona vaccine, USA

"I would like to be called an African just like every living Black person in the universe is African. This is my origin and I want to respect the belief...just like the legendary reggae star Peter Tosh sang, "No matter where you come from, as long as you are a Black man, you're an African". Nigeria is part of Africa and I'm a proud African son."

— Dr. Emeka Obiozor, Department of Exceptionality Programs, Bloomsburg University of Pennsylvania, Bloomsburg, PA 17815 USA

"I think a person from Nigeria should be called Nigerian. Although I am from the Caribbean I want to be identified as a Jamaican. It is my specific country. Since Africa is made up of different countries, then people should be specifically identified as such. People from Italy are not routinely called Europeans. A person from France is referred to as French. So, why should someone from Africa be different? Why should a person from Nigeria not be called Nigerian?"

— **Adelle Haley, US-based Jamaican author of the 2005 book, *Be Still…A Necessary Pill***

As the foregoing *vox pop* has shown, many people from Africa have infectious faith in their African identity, with all its image toxins, and I commend them for it.

After all, about 40 million people in United States of America are called African-Americans, and there is merit in the idea of African countries pooling together in European Union and NAFTA-like ways to promote intra-continental trade and investments in pursuance of post-modern development.

However, pooling together to promote intra-continental trade and investments is not the same as being lumped and limited together as Brand Africa. The latter is hurtful to trade and tourism in Africa's constituent sovereign nations like Nigeria and South Africa as Brand Africa evokes economic insouciance in target markets like America where Mexico, Vietnam and Brazil, for instance, stand on their feet of individual nomenclature, visibility, relevance and competitiveness, hiding under no limiting continental cover.

> *"Brand Africa evokes economic insouciance in target markets like America where Mexico, Vietnam and Brazil, for instance, stand on their feet of individual nomenclature, visibility, relevance and competitiveness, hiding under no limiting continental cover."*

Besides, as mentioned earlier, calling a Nigerian or South African an African is fundamentally devoid of fairness because people from other continents are identified by their national identities, not their continental identities.

People generally convey their values and preferences by words and deeds. One example I often give when talking about personal re-branding is: If you are invited to speak at an event alongside two other speakers and the organizers put you in Motel 6 and put the other two speakers in Marriot, the organizers have simply told you your personal brand is worth less than those of the other two speakers which means you should re-brand yourself to attract the treatment you deserve.

That applies to cities and nations as well, and especially those in Africa, which is why this book is also about re-branding nations on the continent.

Just as every person is a brand – though many people do not see themselves as such, confining their understanding of brands to very visible and strong personal, charity or corporate brands like Wal-Mart, Starbucks, Clinton, Obama and Bono – every city or nation is a brand too because it stands for something in people's minds and eyes. Thus, the difference between city brands like Lagos and Las Vegas or nation brands like China and Nigeria may well be in effective communication, competitive positioning, measurable potency, purposeful resilience and visible dynamism.

A brand is weak or strong, successful or unsuccessful, first, second, third, fourth or last in line, largely dependent on whether it is persistently proactive or reluctantly reactionary. **A successful brand doesn't have to be the creator of the game. It only has to be the one that stays ahead of the game.** A good and strong brand speaks to me of a superbly maintained and expert-driven yellow-colored super cab (instead of a race car) on twists and turns-filled Interstate 80 alongside blue, green and orange-colored super cabs, all seeking the kudos and patronage of ever changing emotional fans who are either quiet, waving and clapping, jumping in or booing by the road sides; a fluid reality that must be observed, measured, compared, guarded and laser-guided to target market appreciation and sustained and incremental patronage or otherwise.

Unfortunately, many city and nation brands in Africa do not operate with such pragmatic understanding and therefore need urgent re-branding. Many of them seem to find refuge in the defective hope that the long-running geo-branding war on them will simply cease one day, thus allowing them to breathe the fresh air of freedom at last. I know it won't unless they do concrete things – many of which I discussed in this book - that will eventually yield desired victory that must be retained.

I believe whenever a Nigerian in America is called an African in keeping with the PIDIC image, Nigeria's urgent need for such a re-branding that would make individuals and businesses around the world give it its due, is greatly illuminated, and this is also true of nationals of other African nations like Gambia, Kenya, DRC, South Africa and others.

Think of it. A Mexican is not called a North American but a Mexican. Properly addressing a Mexican as such brings Mexico to the fore, thus challenging the curiosity of Americans about the Mexican nation and, of course, its consumer products, its many restaurants in American cities and its beautiful tourist city of Cancun which has played host to many Americans. Some will argue that people from Mexico are called Mexicans in America because Mexico, which is part of the North American Free Trade Agreement alongside America and Canada, is not far away like Nigeria. Well, that may be true but Vietnam is far away from the US like Nigeria but Americans don't call Vietnamese Asians. They call them Vietnamese.

Mind you, Vietnam was once seen as an enemy of the US. Americans still talk about The Vietnam War, 1959-1975, with some comparing it to the ongoing Iraq War, but many Americans now go to Vietnam as tourists, importers and investors and Vietnamese products and restaurants are becoming as ubiquitous across America as Chinese products and all-you-can-eat restaurants.

That, you will agree with me, is compelling visibility that helps to shape American public opinion about Brand Vietnam and the Vietnamese people.

Chapter Three

The surface is never deep

You hear it often that a book should not be judged by its cover, which sounds very logical, but the reality on the ground is that most people consciously or unconsciously judge a book by its cover. If it is not appealing to their eyes, if it does not capture their attention in a bookstore, they don't draw near to pick and open it, except it is a book written by a well known political or business leader, a Hollywood superstar or a personal tragedy-catapulted celebrity.

A good book cover is about connecting with people visually and emotionally, and so is a product, socio-political or business event, corporate organization or in this case, a country like China or Nigeria. If it does not look good on the surface, you face the risk of people thinking and saying it is not good. And when one person says - especially in the mass media or at a public or business event – that it is not good, and you do nothing smart about it, others believe it and you are in trouble.

> *"... if you are a Nigerian living outside Nigeria, and especially in countries like America, Canada and United Kingdom, you are always guilty until proven innocent..."*

As stated in a previous chapter, if you are a Nigerian living outside Nigeria, and especially in countries like America, Canada and United Kingdom, you are always guilty until proven innocent by twist of fate. You seem to always live under the erroneous assumption of people around you that you are up to something bad, perhaps because whenever Nigeria is in the news, it is always about advance fee-fraud, fatal plane crash in Nigeria or increased prices at Northern gas stations, **NEVER** about the inestimable contributions of its law-abiding professionals in the educational, health and other sectors of the North or its contributions to global peace keeping and its big brother role to other developing nations. Where is the fairness or balance in that?

In September/October 2007, I waited for the corporate media to add "Nigerian-born" when talking about Professor Ibrahim Gambari, the UN envoy to Myanmar and its Under-Secretary-General for Political Affairs. It never came, but was it surprising? Nothing good was expected to come out of Nigeria and indeed the whole of Africa.

Bad name only

Let me share with you a personal example of how Nigeria shows up in some American discussions. In September 2007, I attended a Washington State advanced exporting course in Tacoma and I must tell you I really loved it because I learned a helpful lot and made some useful contacts. My only problem with the course was that all I heard was about China, India, Japan, Germany, Britain, Mexico and Canada – the ones many believe are important to US trade. The only reference to Nigeria came when a fellow participant, knowing I am Nigerian, expressed concern over letters of "intent" from bogus prospective Nigerian importers, though he started by saying "with deference to Paschal."

Of course, I reacted as diplomatically as I could because while I strongly condemn any act of intended or executed fraud by any Nigerian, the truth is:

(A) Such action – which I totally condemn - is not unique to Nigeria. There are credit card, social security and corporate frauds in America, for instance;

(B) I have received many suspicious fraud-pursuant emails from few bad eggs in countries in the Northern Hemisphere but I ignored or simply deleted them;

(C) The mostly uneducated bad eggs sending such types of emails from Nigeria must be less than 0.005% of Nigeria's population of 150 million; and

(D) In recent years, the Nigerian government has been doing a lot to combat corruption at all levels through its Economic and Financial Crimes Commission (EFCC) though critics say it has largely been directed against political opponents.

Though I am a Nigerian, I also receive but laughingly dismiss such clearly suspect emails because I have no intentions of reaping where I did not sow or defrauding the Nigerian people as the emails clearly propose. I totally condemn these emails because:

(A) they are criminal and immoral;

(B) they hurt the image of Nigeria and millions of its law-abiding people in no little way.

(C) they also shatter lives and destroy families and businesses of victims in the North.

However, I wasn't surprised that nothing else was said at the Tacoma course on Nigeria and other African countries that care about trade and are, in varying degrees, doing a lot to promote and attract trade and investments. People generally say what they feel and they have the right to do so as long as they do not step on the rights of others.

I knew that though many big American businesses like Starbucks, Hershey Foods Corp., M&M Mars and Nestle import their raw materials from African countries like Ethiopia and Ivory Coast, it was not something many Americans would ordinarily know about. I also knew that a good number of prominent African-Americans like Andrew Young and Jesse Jackson have real experiential knowledge of business ready or bubbly African countries like Nigeria, Ghana and South Africa and their ongoing business reforms. But I was at home with the fact that it wasn't their duty to create the much-needed awareness that the continent of Africa is not a large heap of ruins or a lion and monkey-filled jungle of sub-humanity but a continent of 54 countries with hard-working peoples and unsung beckoning opportunities.

So, I ask: Where then are African embassies in Washington DC that should rise up to the challenge of serving as the marketing department of their respective countries - Nigeria, Inc., Ghana, Inc, Mauritius, Inc. or South Africa, Inc., etc?

> *"Where are African embassies in Washington DC that should rise up to the challenge of serving as the marketing department of their respective countries - Nigeria, Inc., Ghana, Inc., Mauritius, Inc. or South Africa, Inc., etc?"*

In trying to find markets for their finished products, manufacturers, distributors and export management companies in the various African countries tend to target big companies like Target, Mattel and Wal-Mart that are in bed with China, India and other Asian countries. This is understandable because of the carrying capacities of such big companies and the opportunity of leveraging from their big brands to attract patronage from other big and even small companies.

Big Company A headquartered in Bentonville accepts to buy Product Q from Mauritius partly because its competitor, Big Company B headquartered in Minneapolis has Product Q on its shelves. Then Small Company Y in Iowa City chooses to stock Product Q as well because it wants to be seen as offering the same products as Big Company A and Big Company B.

You know how that goes. Yet, small and medium sized companies may be the most strategic partners for introducing Made-in-Nigeria or Made-in-Mauritius products to the American market. Why? They have little or no red tape. The decision to buy a product could be made without delay by an individual. Small businesses could be reached through the chambers of commerce in most American cities. For instance, a South African software company could carefully choose 5 pilot cities in America to launch a small business accounting software, the point of departure being to make powerful product presentations in relevant meetings of the chambers of commerce in those cities. If attendees appreciate the benefits they could derive from the product, they are likely to go to their nearest office supplies stores and ask for the software, thus creating the enabling environment for the office supplies stores to order the software.

This is somewhat like independent book publishing. Big bookstores and even independent bookstores don't stock a book by an independent publisher (who has not published a celebrity and has not struck a deal with a major distributor) until it is listed in Books in Print and Ingram database and at least five people come in to ask for the book.

Underperforming AGOA again!

I have argued and will continue to argue that because of the PIDIC image I explained in Chapter One, many people in the North can hardly imagine African countries having any meaningful thing to do with global trade and tourism. And such change-needy mindset relates to the African Growth and Opportunity Act (AGOA) as well.

Though US AGOA imports from sub-Saharan African countries in 2006 were put at about $44.2 billion, most of it were traditional imports like oil and gas, platinum, diamonds and gold (natural resources, raw materials), not export diversification items like food products, automobiles, iron and steel, clothing and chemicals that would further promote economic growth and help better the living conditions of ordinary citizens in sub-Saharan Africa. About 6400 products are covered by AGOA and African countries like South Africa and Nigeria have many little known finished products to meet the needs of the American market.

> *"Whenever and wherever there are Africa-centric business expos in the US, all you see are shea butter, wood carvings, beads and tie and dye, which honestly do not have strong crossover appeal and power."*

Why then have raw materials remained the major import focus of American businesses? How about this first reason? Whenever and wherever there are Africa-centric business expos in the US, all you see are shea butter, wood carvings, beads and tie and dye, which honestly do not have strong crossover appeal and power. They appeal mainly to people of African origin who do not buy plenty, not to Whites, Asians, Hispanics, Jewish, etc. Chinese entrepreneurs, in contrast, would have showcased household accents and decors, kitchen wares, Northern market-friendly shoes, belts, leather bags, plastic bowls and rose flowers – all items with mass and all-year-round appeal which, I know, are also manufactured in a number of African countries. Why don't companies manufacturing aforementioned products and others exhibit at relevant trade shows in the US? Why do they allow the impression that entrepreneurship in African countries are all about shea butter, wood carvings, beads and tie and dye to thrive? These items are very unlikely to command wide and meaningful patronage to significantly impact African economies. They do not have strong cross-over appeal.

Over 60% of America's businesses are small businesses creating 60-80 of net new jobs in the country. According to Dr. Chad Moutray, chief economist of U.S. Small Business Administration's Office of Advocacy, "Small business drives the American economy." **(1)** Many of these businesses are missing out on the many business opportunities in the real Africa because they are understandably oblivious of them or have been scared by lopsided news reports on the besieged continent mostly populated by Blacks.

While big companies know a lot about African countries but remain pursuant of their interest of keeping them sources of raw materials, these small businesses, I believe, are more likely to tap into the huge opportunities in Africa's export market when exposed to such opportunities.

When small businesses in America get to know the real Africa, especially sub-Saharan Africa – its peoples, business opportunities, manufacturing activities, export products, etc – they will be attracted to the numerous export products therein. In other words, many of America's small businesses are more likely to tap into AGOA than the big businesses, and therefore urgently need to know that what they have been sourcing in Asian nations may be better sourced in African countries from Nigeria to South Africa.

In my travels and professional engagements across the US, I have come across small business owners that know next to nothing about AGOA formulated by their own government let alone the attractive business opportunities in sub-Saharan African countries like Nigeria. Incidentally, some of these AGOA-oblivious business owners are well meaning African-Americans. The number of black-owned businesses reportedly grew more than four times the national rate from 1997 to 2002, with 25% revenue increase to about $89 billion. That tells me African-American businesses could and should play a key role in the promotion of Made-in-Ghana, Made-in-Kenya or Made-in-Nigeria goods, as the case may be.

I often like to tell or remind people that one in every six Blacks in the world is said to be a Nigerian. This is important because the US has about 40 million Blacks from Atlanta and Detroit to Waterloo, which could mean that a disregard for Nigeria is a disregard for these Blacks.

So, I recommend (a) creative public awareness campaign, (b) continuous see-for-yourself engagements with US Small Business Administration, World

Trade Centers and chambers of commerce across the country, and (c) active participation in strategic vertical and horizontal trade shows.

I do not pretend to be a copywriting expert but I believe if Nigeria, for instance, really wants to capture relevant attention and inspire positive action towards its quality but poorly marketed consumer products, it should, among other things, run powerful ads in select American media outlets, including new media, that say things like:

> **If you are like me...**
> You will learn something new every day. Someone just told me the African nation of Nigeria probably manufactures more top quality consumer products than Florida, Kansas, Michigan, Iowa, Texas, Illinois and Virginia put together. Can you believe it? I didn't until I visited **PutDomainNameHere.com.** Visit this site now and see for yourself.

People simply like comparison. They like relating the known to the unknown. They also like to discover new exciting things. So, if well produced and properly placed with requisite understanding of the target audience, the ad could easily capture the attention of, and help to broaden the horizon of many "Chinese products-only" importers across the US. It could also – and this is very important - effectively challenge many American journalists, broadcasters and TV commentators **who hardly admit their inversed objectivity about the real Nigeria** (and other African countries) to dig deep and unearth the facts they have been running away from – that good products and good people come from Nigeria (and other African countries) too.

When they finally ascertain the quantity and quality of Nigerian consumer products by experiencing – even if reluctantly - the other Nigeria, they will be faced with the glaring challenge of doing for Nigeria what they have been doing for India, China, Vietnam, South Korea and Japan, among other Asian nations, with their busy professional cameras and computer keyboards. Thus, they could for the first time show footages of Nigerian factories churning out tangible quality consumer products as well as Nigerian corporate executives on the cutting edge of strategic marketing and brand management like their American counterparts, instead of religiously showing footages of Nigerian scams, slums and scavengers.

Another well produced and placed ad could say something like:

> **Worried about high gas prices?**
> John and Julia here were worried too until they decided to do something about it. They visited **PutDomainNameHere.com** and couldn't help wondering what took them so long. It's free information. So, what do you have to lose?
>
> Logon to **PutDomainNameHere.com** and discover for yourself what you have been missing.

It could get quality attention and contribute significantly in stimulating a transformation of thought about Nigeria and other countries of Africa collectively and customarily seen as mere objects of self-gratifying pity, pittance or prejudice.

Safe for trade, tourism?

For starters, let me point out that I love ecotourism, and I find the Kwesi Hanson-owned Hans Cottage Botel in Cape Coast Ghana (www.hansbotel.com) and Makasutu Culture Forest in The Gambia (www.makasutu.com) as my favorite ecotourist sites. They are charmingly authentic and remarkably re-generating. When I savored them years ago as a travel writer, the convoluted world was safely locked outside as I emptied myself in unforgettable blitz of tranquility and treasured gratitude. How I wish their beautiful websites would be made to become highly visible on major search engines like Google, Yahoo and AOL on relevant eco-tourism keywords so more people searching on the Internet for beyond-the-ordinary destinations for their next vacations would easily discover them and be encouraged to reach out and enjoy them.

But did I hear you ask: Are sub-Saharan African countries like Ghana and The Gambia safe for trade and tourism? Yes, they truly are. Besides, the last time I checked, Iraq was one of the most unsafe places on the face of the earth. The 2007 Failed States Index of the Foreign Policy magazine and the Fund for Peace ranks Iraq as the second most un-stable country in the world, behind Sudan (2) that has been goldmine to China. Yet, thousands of Americans, Australians and others go to Iraq as private contractors on the lure of hundreds of dollars in daily wages and fat reconstruction and security contracts.

> *"So, the cry about Nigeria has really not been about safety.*
> *If it has been about safety, what about Iraq?"*

So, the cry about Nigeria has really not been about safety. If it has been about safety, what about Iraq where you can hardly walk or drive on the streets of Baghdad without being blown up by insurgents or terrorists? The reason many lovely main street Americans are not visiting, trading with and investing in Nigeria is that they have unfortunately been made to believe the Nigeria that exports oil and quality labor to America is entirely up to no good.

I like the Asian country of India but get this: "According to the latest official figures, a woman is raped every half-hour in India. Last year, there were more than 18,000 rapes in the country, and these are only the reported cases. Activists suspect the number is much higher as many women don't report attacks to police, fearing harassment or social stigma."(3) Yet, many Americans tour and import a lot of goods from the Indian nation that cable TV images market as irresistible for trade and investment while projecting Nigeria as mendicant of global aid but deserving trade and investment aversion. I am not saying India is bad for business. It isn't. I am only saying there are safety concerns and fears over every country under the sun, such as the risk of women visitors being raped in India, or the likelihood of Americans receiving fraud-driven emails from Nigeria.

The Middle East is still the world's most volatile region. Yet many people go there for pilgrimage, business and diplomatic validation. No week passes without a major violent incident there but people still go there for various reasons. Do you know why? They have very powerful media and lobbyist support in the US and other Northern countries who persistently and effectively plead their causes. African countries are not that "lucky". **Remember when many American Blacks, motivated by the glaring fact that Whites were involved, joined their kith and kin in Africa in the fight to drub apartheid? The Darfur genocide in Sudan has somehow proven that was a fluke.**

There are probably as many violent crimes in American cities of New Orleans, St. Louis and Detroit as in sub-Saharan African cities of Lagos, Nairobi and Johannesburg. So, trumpeting trade and tourism

73

hindering crimes in sub-Saharan African cities is either quintessentially disingenuous, a signature product of creative fear or simply a carnival game of geopolitical superiority. Yet, I love America and Americans which is why I live in America.

Lest I forget, tourist destinations like The Gambia, knowing the American public and corporate media are waging deserved war against pedophilia, can launch out to earn quality media attention and arouse public interest with ads that say things like:

Making plans for your next vacation?
You've got to put Gambia on your list.
A nation of genuine warmth, Gambia
has been memorable fun to millions
of decent tourists, but no-go area for pedophiles.
Visit **Gambianopedophiles.com**

Though American and Canadian pedophiles have found the Asian country of Thailand their favorite destination, British, Belgian, Dutch and German pedophiles have also thought of the tiny African country of The Gambia as a favorite sex tourist destination though the Gambia government and the country's growing tourist sector have been making giant efforts to repel them. Wondering what their attraction is? Poverty, of course! Pedophilic tourists exploit poverty to the brim. They love to prey on the poor – just like some celebrities and corporate media giants.

Chapter Four

From virtual accents to verbal pity

The picture painted in the preceding chapters presents a clear-cut challenge for professionals from these African countries, including their arguably marketing-challenged armchair diplomats in Washington DC where the branding savvy wins big.

African countries of Nigeria, Ghana, Kenya, South Africa and others have been good sources of professionals like medical doctors, pharmacists, nurses, journalists, software engineers and accountants for America. Needless to say many Americans will find it difficult to associate Brand Africa with such highly skilled manpower.

One reason Americans don't associate African countries with highly skilled labor is that many of the aforementioned professionals labor beyond measure to speak with American accent in utter reflection of their "I belong at last" thrust or in fulfillment of their understandable desire to impress their relatives and peers back home. They reason that speaking with such borrowed accent would make people they come across think they are African-Americans, not people born on the continent of Africa. This is disturbing and detestable because when people think of them as African-Americans, the African country of their birth is completely shut out. And so does the African continent since many Americans would call a non borrowed accent-laden Nigerian an African, instead of a Nigerian.

> *"They reason that speaking with such borrowed accent would make people they come across think they are African-Americans, not people born on the continent of Africa. This is disturbing and detestable because when people think of them as African-Americans, the African country of their birth is completely shut out."*

But make no mistake about it. I love African-Americans and have African-American friends and associates but those truisms do not give me (or any other Black person born in a sub-Saharan African country) the justification to pretend to be an African-American just to fit in. So you ask: What then should naturalized Nigerians, Gambians, Kenyans and Senegalese in America be called? I would simply say Nigerian-Americans, Gambian-Americans, Kenyan-Americans and Senegalese-Americans, respectively. Collectively, they should be called Black-Americans because that's what they are.

For the Chinese, it's about marketing and sales

The Chinese have taught us that if there are situations that allow for speaking with borrowed American or British accent, they are the ones that help boost exports. Here are two ready examples:

A. Many Chinese newscasters and show presenters on CCTV9 – the 24-7 Chinese satellite English TV broadcast around the world - use borrowed accent to try and capture the attention and interest of their international audience; and

B. Many Chinese manufacturers' representatives like Cyber Import

(www.CyberImport.com.cn) that target
Internet importers tend to use borrowed accent to capture the interest and trust of
overseas importers as well. These savvy
businesses are mostly owned and run by
Chinese people who had lived or studied in
the North but returned home to help boost
China's export economy by setting up manufacturers' representation businesses or export management companies (EMCs) with
visually and navigationally powerful online
operations.

On the websites of these cyber export facilitators are
usually American, Australian, Brazilian and British
phone numbers, which, when you dial, connect you
directly to them in China and they speak to you with
American, British or Australian accent, as the case
may be. That, in my opinion, tends to instill some
measure of confidence in you, especially if you have
not been to China before or have been having some
anxiety or trepidation about importing from China.

And that makes me wonder how many American or
Canadian-based borrowed accent speaking people
from Nigeria to Namibia have found it a desideratum to boost their country's exports by setting up
EMCs, manufacturers' representation businesses and
export training consultancies, which they could do
alongside their 9am-5pm jobs in America or Canada,
with the help of the Internet and telecommunication.

They must be few, although I know there are many borrowed accent speaking people, including international trade specialists, in the reformed and booming banking sector across Africa.

You can then understand why mine has been a daily temptation, a ceaseless pressure to speak with borrowed accent. This is more so when some people in corporate cocoons in America and Canada demonstrate to me in unmistakable terms that their biases trump my willingness to buy their cars and trucks for export, that a ready buyer like me with a Nigerian accent is justifiably unwelcome. Or better put, that they believe there is no need for cars and trucks in the Nigeria of their imagination, which unknown to them, has **six** car plants, one of them being ANAMMCO in which the DaimlerChrysler they know, has a 40% stake.

> *"...they believe there is no need for cars and trucks in the Nigeria of their imagination, which unknown to them, has <u>six</u> car plants, one of them being ANAMMCO in which the <u>DaimlerChrysler</u> they know, has a 40% stake."*

As recently as December 2006, ASD Motors, a Nigerian-owned car distribution company, paid US$31.98 million for a 54.87% stake in Peugeot Automotive Nigeria (PAN), the country's largest car maker. Besides, the Nigerian government has rolled out a car loan program for its employees to buy PAN-made cars and thus boost domestic car sales.

The obvious challenge however is that, as I noted in Chapter One, many Nigerian roads are poorly maintained, its railway system collapsed decades ago, the waterways are grossly underutilized and domestic flights are expensive, thus putting heavy pressure on the roads which are flooded with more affordable imported "second-hand" cars especially popular brands like Toyota Camry and Honda Accord.

But back to the issue of immigrant conformity, as I consider the uncompromising accent of almost all the Chinese and Indians I have encountered, and the Census Bureau statistics that put the undoubtedly entrepreneurial people of Asian extraction as having the highest household income in the country despite their foreign accent, I elect to hold tenaciously to my accent. In 2006, **"Asian households had the highest median income at $64,200, followed by non-Hispanic white ($52,400), Hispanic ($37,800) and black ($32,000) households." (1)**

If the Chinese and the Indians retain their accents in America and still make a lot of money, it is because they are not oblivious of the fact that trade, technology and branding drive the world, not accents. Chinese entrepreneurs set up all-you-can-eat restaurants across America, serving people of all races and creeds, without changing their accents or Americanizing their menus. In fact, many Americans now take Mandarin language classes in classrooms or on the Internet.

> *"If the Chinese and the Indians retain their accents in America and still make a lot of money, it is because they are not oblivious of the fact that trade, technology and branding drive the world, not accents."*

Koreans clearly dominate the Black hair product market across America without attempting to make their Black American customers see them as Black Americans, which they are not. An enterprise-minded person from Nepal, Syria, Mongolia or Lebanon arrives in Detroit Michigan or Chicago Illinois and works for barely two years in a grocery store owned by one of his compatriots. Before you know it, his compatriots and friends collate money to augment his healthy personal savings (because he does not buy all-you-can-see with credit cards), helping him set up his own grocery store. And in two to three years, he has not only opened three, four branches of his grocery store but also helped fellow compatriots open their own stores in Detroit and other American cities. Yet, he remains faithful to his cultural heritage, to his identity, while making a lot of money. Isn't that very instructive?

I believe that while the aforementioned professionals from Nigeria and other African countries do have the right to speak with all the borrowed accents they can find, the risk is that of still remaining victims of the intense geo-branding war that discounts their personal brands – that is, if they see themselves as brands in the first place.

Or how else should I put it when some of them see a desideratum in religiously dressing-to-belong in Chinese-made but American-styled apparels and live in credit card-propelled ways that seem to suggest no modicum of connection with the continent of Africa? Is it about the good old cliché of "doing as the Romans do while in Rome?" I don't think so.

My take is that their attitude has all to do with the truism that it is not "cool" or "sexy" to identify with Africa these days unless you are a fundraising global nonprofit brand like the Clinton Foundation, Feed the Children, Red Cross and Bono or celebrity child adopters like UNHCR goodwill ambassador, Angelina Jolie, and pop star, Madonna. Thank goodness that former US Vice President, Nobel Laureate Al Gore, chose to boost his brand value internationally with his passionate global warming campaign instead of Africa's Poverty, Instability, Disease, Illiteracy and Corruption (PIDIC).

Big questions for Big charities, Big celebrities

Many big charities and big celebrities – as helpful as they seem to have been on issues of poverty and disease in African countries – contribute immensely to the condescending way people in America see and relate to Africa and immigrants from Africa. They routinely exploit the power of select TV images in their fundraising binge, and in raising the so-called awareness about poverty and disease in Africa, tend to draw greater attention and wider support for their TV-driven brands. I have seen senior staff members of big charities in Africa live in such disturbing lavish that insult the compassion and intelligence of their lovely American donors, and I believe that big celebrities that visit select African countries do so mainly to boost their brand value through cause marketing or rather despair marketing.

Believe it or not, it is not that they truly identify with the cause of the poor on the beleaguered continent but because Brand Africa requires and attracts it, people generally believe Africa is quintessentially mendicant of pity, and despair marketing is very visibly rewarding.

> *"...people generally believe Africa is quintessentially mendicant of pity, and despair marketing is very visibly rewarding."*

Paris Hilton is now turning to Rwanda – an African country that was seemingly etched into the memory of Americans by the 2004 movie Hotel Rwanda – in an attempt to re-brand herself or is it, as she told E! News, because "There's so much need in that area, and I feel like if I go, it will bring more attention to what people can do to help"? **(2)**

Great! Rwanda miraculously grabbed her attention overnight. Didn't she watch or hear about Hotel Rwanda in 2004? When will these media-exalted people realize that African countries like Rwanda need trade and investments, not celebrity reverse sympathy and well packaged PR events? When will they realize that a $14 million or even $1 million revolving loan fund for rural female farmers in Ivory Coast, DRC, Liberia, Rwanda, Angola, Sierra Leone and Ethiopia will do more to transform lives in those African countries than their calculated celebrity visits and obvious PR events?

Unlike Oprah that built a school in South Africa with her own money, acting with the courage of her conviction that better education will change lives of beneficiaries, these here and there stars raise mere emotional dusts and sensationalize and massage the problem for media glory or make-belief self-redemption.

I am still waiting patiently to hear of one crowd-pulling Hollywood celebrity or sweet-talking TV personality who will set up a revolving loan fund for people in just one city in an African country, giving out a mere $200 per person in revolving loans that will do more for a peanut farmer than their celebrity handshake amid a flurry of paparazzi. No amount of celebrity photo-ops and make-me-feel-good "goodwill" visits can achieve as much as well managed micro-financing in African countries.

> *"Unlike Oprah that built a school in South Africa with her own money, acting with the courage of her conviction that better education will change lives of beneficiaries, these here and there stars raise mere emotional dusts and sensationalize and massage the problem for media glory or make-belief self-redemption. "*

These celebrities are rich enough to put their money bags where their "feel good" verbal and media pity is. If they are not all about their personal brand promotion in the media, they will go into life-changing projects like micro-lending, which millions of working poor, especially women across Africa need to better their lives and those of their families.

Remember the Muhammad Yunus' Nobel Prize-winning Grameen Bank in Bangladesh? It is working in Bangladesh, despite tornado-like criticisms from sources conveniently allergic to such non traditional banking that has no huge profit thrust. It has been working for hundreds of years in countries like Nigeria albeit on an informal peer-like scale that is far-removed from the news worthiness of the northern corporate media.

Providing cheaper anti-retroviral drugs may be the cherry-picked focus of some global personal brands because it massages the problem, gains the masterminds northern media blitz and keeps the continent where multinational corporations want it to remain. But micro-lending sites like MyC4.com, Kiva.com and eBay-owned Microplace are tackling the problem from its roots and truly changing lives. Less known MyC4.com founders, Tim Vang and Mads Kjær, are probably practically and meaningfully changing more lives in Uganda than all the Hollywood stars have tried to do across the African continent with their personal brand projecting and surface-scratching visits, handshakes, child adoptions and TV glare. Why? Micro-lending is the thrust of independence but aid, as good as it appears, is the trench of dependence which will not bring about desired development in African countries.

Chapter Five

Suspect media, 'distant' kins and Brand Africa

As I include in this chapter few examples of the ignoble role of corporate media in boosting international trade and tourism for some countries and blocking them for others, I am mindful of the fact that I have been part of the media profession which boasts many fine and experienced professionals not only in the North but also in developing nations.

My problem, however, is that if TV news on American presidential elections warrants footages of the magnificent White House, why shouldn't news on elections in Nigeria warrant footages of the very scenic Aso Rock Presidential Villa? Instead, they show audiences scary footages of slums or better put, very congested, poorly planned cities with large refuse heaps and heavy human and vehicular traffic – just to tout and reinforce the Brand Africa image of Nigeria as "backward" and worthy of serving no other purpose in world trade but as supplier of raw materials.

'Bad things only' media coverage

I remember when the very popular US Senator Barack Obama (who later became a presidential candidate) paid his August 2006 visit to his father's home country of Kenya, the focus of the Northern corporate media was on Kibera, a slum said to be home to over 600, 000 people, in keeping with Brand Africa.

This is how the British Broadcasting Corporation (BBC) put it: "Mr. Obama walked through rubbish and sewage as he toured Kibera, the slum home to at least 600,000 people, many without jobs or legal title to the land they inhabit." **(1)** While this "just as expected" portrayal could lure donor-fatigued NGOs many of whose staff live in such stupendous luxury in Africa that demands donor concerns, it will scare many prospective importers, tourists and investors except those exclusively interested in raw materials.

Chapter Five: Suspect media, 'distant' kins and Brand Africa

In February 2007, Kenyan-born CNN Africa correspondent, Jeff Koinange, did a "Big guns, big oil collide in Nigeria" story on CNN that painted Nigeria as very unsafe for foreign investors and workers. **(2)** Who knows? May be, the report could have won CNN a coveted media award.

> *"I felt relieved that Nigeria was beginning to see itself as a nation brand whose value could go further south because of a negative media message..."*

Shortly after CNN ran the story, the then Nigerian information and communications minister, Frank Nweke Jr., fired back at CNN, saying the story "utterly disregards the most elementary principle of journalism because no government official was interviewed." **(3)**

He went on to posit that the story sent the wrong message to the international community, created panic and portrayed Nigeria "as a country in perpetual crises." **(4)** Such a timely reaction, I must state, was very much unlike Nigeria, which would have kept mute, ignoring its right of prompt response, as its name was dragged through the international mud. I felt relieved that Nigeria was beginning to see itself as a nation brand whose value could go further south because of a negative media message on a global media giant like CNN. After all, a nation brand worth media pounding is certainly worth vigorous protection and promotion by its custodian. Few months after the timely Nigerian government rebuttal, Koinange was reportedly fired.

Are there problems in the Niger Delta region of Nigeria? Yes, there are, and I strongly call on the Nigerian government to administer requisite justice to the area and other parts of the country where people are denied their dues. But the story forcefully struck at the heart of Nigeria's major export, oil, without simultaneously presenting the views of the other side, the Nigerian side. It brandished Nigeria not only as unsafe but as very highly prohibitive, which is unfair and very inimical to Nigeria's economic well being and by implication the well being of millions of Nigerians, even though the Nigerian government has not been doing enough to address such problems as those of its Niger Delta region.

I have been watching CNN for a long time. I remember frequently getting my international talking points from CNN, BBC and the Internet as a newspaper editor in the touristy country of Republic of The Gambia. Today, I have widely broadened my sources from Iowa's KCRG and KWWL to Link TV, Free Speech TV and, of course, China Central Television (CCTV9), which means I still get my news from CNN, BBC and more frequently the Internet though I do not agree with all the things I see and hear.

I admire the style and wit of Situation Room gentleman Wolf Blitzer, report-it-like-it-is Michael Ware, straight-in-your-face Jack Cafferty, Anderson Cooper of the "Keeping Them Honest" refrain and Rick Sanchez who keeps relevant issues "Out in the Open." I also like to follow international dispatches from 9-Emmy Award winning CNN chief international correspondent, Christiane Amanpour. But I must say I was disappointed that her special documentary, "Where have all the parents gone?" gave an unmistakable impression of the African tourist destination of Kenya as a place bereft of good things – tarred roads, high rise buildings, electricity, cars, boulevards, educated and healthy people, just name it. I was very disappointed.

> *"If you don't respond promptly to a media attack, people in their target audience will believe it as true, and more media attacks will follow, pounding you beyond repair..."*

She or her editors and producers apparently packaged the documentary to conform to the Brand Africa of utter despair, rural squalor and hopelessness that scares tourists, investors and international traders. It is either that the footages that would have suggested anything to the contrary were carefully removed or that the cameramen made sure good houses, roads, cars, colleges and well dressed ordinary citizens were not captured by their cameras. With such selective pitiful or prejudice-evoking images shown again and again on the powerful global network, CNN, how could people in America think of Kenya when they need to import or export goods or take a safari vacation? As far as I know, the images purely served fundraising global NGO brands, and not the interest of the Kenyan nation which has reportedly made itself more open for real international business.

My long involvement with the media profession has told me silence in the face of media attack – even in its most subtle form – is an invitation for more media attacks. If you don't respond promptly to a media attack, people in their target audience will believe it as true, and more media attacks will follow, pounding you beyond repair. That's why big countries, big corporations and savvy personal brands like Trump waste no time in firing back and firing back well when a media attack is unleashed on them. Unfortunately, most African countries hiding under Brand Africa have shown that they are easily intimi-

dated by international media attacks disguised as bal-
anced reporting, and only hope and pray the attacks
will cease as they continue to bleed from their attendant visible socio-political and economic wounds.
The time has come for radical change in their international media and public relations.

Thus, one way to dismantle Brand Africa – the
brand people see through carefully shot and projected TV images of Poverty, Instability, Disease,
Illiteracy and Corruption – is for SANE countries
(Africa's economic powerhouses of South Africa,
Algeria, Nigeria and Egypt) to set up their own
strong, globally accessed 24-7 cable news network to
plead their cause and those of other African nations
on the airwaves. Why? For geopolitical and business
reasons, no existing global news network is actively
and consistently pleading their cause now, and we
live in a visually-driven world where TV programs
and movies do a lot to shape public opinions and
actions or inactions.

> "...one way to dismantle Brand Africa – the brand people see through carefully shot and projected TV images of Poverty, Instability, Disease, Illiteracy and Corruption – is for SANE countries (Africa's economic powerhouses of South Africa, Algeria, Nigeria and Egypt) to set up their own strong, globally accessed 24-7 cable news network to plead their cause and those of other African nations on the airwaves."

But I believe media campaign alone will not do it for African countries, especially if not backed up with consumer product diplomacy as exemplified by China and Japan or a Ghana-like homecoming campaign targeting African-Americans and others who want to see African countries of their choice or DNA confirmation as home.

Ghana, a stable African country I have visited several times, has been successful in attracting African-American tourists, home-comers and investors. I **commend those African-Americans who demonstrate their love for sub-Saharan Africa** through heartfelt pilgrimages, viable business investments, holding meetings and conventions in sub-Saharan African cities from Abuja and Accra to Nairobi and Johannesburg, playing good hosts to legal immigrants from Ethiopia to Liberia and speaking up for sub-Saharan Africa in the face of international injustice, humiliation or hypocrisy as in the ongoing Darfur Genocide. I have come across some of them both in Ghanaian capital city of Accra and American cities like Detroit.

In Lathrup Village Michigan is Robin Wright King, MBA, African-American author of the well received 2007 book, *Papa Was A Rolling Stone: A Daughter's Journey To Forgiveness*, who told me she truly loves her kith and kin living in or immigrating from sub-Saharan Africa.

In her words, "I think African Americans can be proud of Africa today, yesterday and in the future because it is the land of our heritage. Africa is like a mother to its children, always there, always nurturing, always forgiving and always extending its open arms to come back home. Africa like any other continent has experienced atrocities from within and without, yet she still stands like a strong unyielding mother." **(5)**

She goes on to state, "I am proud of my African heritage and always intrigued by those who can proudly proclaim their birth place to be Africa. We have much to be proud of and have a greater insight to the extraordinary culture of Africa as it is portrayed via the Africa Channel instead of the white media which will show only the challenges faced by Africa. As we continue to pursue and be exposed to the 'real' Africa, I expect that our enthusiasm and interest will only grow." **(6)**

Why some African-Americans disown Africa

While I commend Author Robin Wright King for her kind perspective, I must observe that there are African-Americans who demonstrate in words and deeds that they do not want to have anything to do with countries on the African continent, unlike most Irish-Americans, Italian-Americans, Indian-Americans and Chinese-Americans I have come across who are infectiously proud to identify with countries of their original extraction.

May be, it is because such African-Americans have not yet established by DNA the specific country on the African continent they originated from. The genetic testing project, the African-American DNA Roots Project, founded in 2001, could make a great difference in this regard.

May be, they are still reeling from the psychological wounds of trans-Atlantic slavery in which their fore-

bears were forcefully kidnapped from their organic
farms and spacious environmentally friendly homes
in self-reliant traditional African societies and
brought to the New World to live in inhumane conditions.

May be, they consider it unforgivable that those African societies had succumbed to the superior fire-
power of the kidnappers from the Northern Hemisphere who were in Hurricane Katrina-like need of
unwilling far-fetched laborers.

Nonetheless, my deep-seated interactions with some
African-Americans and my keen observation of their
disposition to me have made me to conclude it is
mostly because the Nigerian nation of my extraction
is not the technologically vibrant and economically
prosperous China or the successfully IT-branded
Ireland they would have liked it to be.

I strongly believe if sub-Saharan Africa was like
Western Europe or South East Asia, millions of African-Americans would have been living, investing in
or trading with sub-Saharan African countries especially under the seemingly under-utilized African
Growth and Opportunity Act, with all its loopholes.

If African countries like the Ellen Johnson-Sirleaf-
led Liberia (founded with US government support in
1847 by African-Americans who called themselves
Americo-Liberians) were enviable economic suc-

cesses on the world stage, African-American business and political leaders would be paying glowing, incessant tributes to ideas, ideals and achievements of Liberian extraction in their speeches.

> *"...if sub-Saharan Africa was like Western Europe or South East Asia, millions of African-Americans would have been living, investing in or trading with sub-Saharan African countries..."*

If Ghana, South Africa and Uganda had global brands, African-American captains of industry whose eyes are fixed on China, India and Japan would be frequenting industrial and trading hubs in them on mutually beneficial trade missions. They don't.

If Nigeria, Democratic Republic of Congo and Angola were not as missing-in-action as they are in main street America, African-American talk show hosts would have been trumpeting the many notable Black achievers from Abuja to Johannesburg. The Black press in USA would have been painting a realistic positive picture of the remarkable Botswanan socio-political and economic story, the lovely Namibian industrial voyage, the Ghanaian political stability, the Nigerian apron strings-free big brother role among developing nations and the irresistible Kenyan and Gambian tourist attractions. African-American celebrities would have been outdoing one another in owning vacation homes and celebrating their anniversaries in beautiful cities across sub-Saharan Africa.

You guessed right! They don't do it because misbranded Nigeria is not the mighty Japan with Toyota, Honda and Sony to parade. They don't do it because touristy Republic of The Gambia to which *Roots* author Alex Haley traced his ancestry is not the economic giant, China, which boasts Chinese restaurants in any viable city around the world.

I often tell people I believe Chinese restaurants, not Wal-Mart, are the best measures of viable cities to establish their small and medium scale businesses. Thus, if they don't find Chinese restaurants in a city – with Whites, Blacks and Hispanics eating with Chinese chopsticks and attempting to speak permissible pedestrian Mandarin – they should not bother to take the city serious because Chinese restaurants go where the action is, they operate where good business opportunities exist.

But more importantly, Chinese buffet restaurants and Chinese movies featuring Jacky Chan and Jet Li have really been the doorway to Chinese tourism and trade, and indeed part of the best diplomats of China around the world.

Many other countries have their own best diplomats in mostly global consumer products and services as well as corporate brands that people in their target markets love to invite into their lives; products, services and corporate brands that contribute very immensely, for instance, in making and sustaining America's economic supremacy in the world:

Sweden – Volvo, IKEA, Nobel Prize

United Kingdom – Lloyd's

Switzerland – Nescafe, Rolex, Omega, Nestle, Credit Suisse

Finland – Nokia

Russia - Vodka

Denmark – Maersk Line

Japan – Toyota, Honda and Sony

America – Coke, Hollywood movies, Microsoft, IBM, eBay, Amazon.com, Google, Disney World, McDonald's, Nike, CNN

Chapter Five: Suspect media, 'distant' kins and Brand Africa

Germany – BMW, Mercedes Benz, AGFA, Beck's

South Korea – Samsung

Nigeria - ?

South Africa - ?

Sierra Leone - ?

Kenya - ?

Ghana - ?

Gambia - ?

Botswana - ?

Uganda - ?

Liberia - ?

As you must have noticed, the African countries mentioned above do not have global consumer product or service brands that could help a lot in changing the negative perception of them and, of course, boosting their economies through trade. None of them has a global news brand like China's CCTV9, America's CNN or Britain's BBC unobtrusively pleading its cause in the homes and offices of TV audiences in target countries. None of them has global city brands like India's Bangalore (IT), and America's Detroit (motor city, most Africa-friendly city), Hollywood (movies, celebrities), Las Vegas (casinos, entertainment), Washington DC (top flight diplomacy, White House), New York (Wall Street, UN Headquarters) and Orlando (Disney World) which are subsets of the mighty Brand America.

"My primary school-going nieces and nephews in Nigerian cities of Apapa and Badagry can tell you what each of these American cities is known for. Why? They watch CNN in their homes."

My primary school-going nieces and nephews in Nigerian cities of Apapa and Badagry can tell you what each of the aforementioned American cities is known for. Why? They watch CNN in their homes. They watch Hollywood and Nollywood (popular Nigerian digital) movies in their own homes. They read books about beautiful things in America in their own homes. They have internet access in their own homes. They speak good English. They even call on the regular phone and speak with me in Iowa. They live in Nigeria. But can their counterparts in America, especially those born of immigrant Nigerian parents, tell you Apapa is home to one of Africa's biggest ports and Badagry is a serene coastal city on Nigeria's border with Benin Republic that was home to its first Christian mission in the 1840s? I don't think so. Who wants to identify with PIDIC?

Thank God Liberian president Ellen Johnson-Sirleaf is held in high esteem in elite circles in America perhaps because she is Africa's first elected female president, Harvard-educated, belongs to the Alpha Kappa Alpha Sorority, has been featured on the powerful Oprah show, has addressed a joint session of US Congress and was in 2006 named 51st most powerful woman in the world by Forbes magazine. Thus, she readily comes to mind when people think of Liberia that was once under the chokehold of Charles Taylor.

But think of what could happen if, for instance, some Kenyans start a Virtual Safari franchise, some Tanzanians create and widely distribute a Mount Kilimanjaro Climb Game, and some Nigerians start an organic products chain, which may well become their countries' best diplomats in a world where the branding savvy gets it all.

Why those three options? I have thought of many more, but I reasoned that entertainment loving Americans could relate well to a properly branded and managed virtual safari or outdoor-themed game just as America's rapidly growing population of organic product consumers could relate well to a properly branded and managed organic products chain, with dependable and coherent supply chain and distribution.

Chapter Six

Geo-branding shock and awe

There are double standards in many things we value or pretend to value in life – access to socio-political and economic opportunities, validation and application of family values, taxation, allocation and disbursement of public funds, provision of essential services, news coverage and even dispensation of justice.

Even-handedness in most facets of the human society could at best be a myth, a mental abstract, a political palliative, a convenient retreat from stark reality.

Though an understandable non-issue on elite golf courses, Wall Street and the Capitol, countless single mothers devoid of health insurance, student loan-

wearied youths, and the very many victims of fore-
closures across the United States certainly feel every
inch of it.

Yet, they may not feel it as intensely as many legal
immigrants from sub-Saharan Africa who, thanks to
the carefully selected and passionately projected TV
images of sub-Saharan African squalor and disease,
are seen as toxic escapees of sub-humanity.

> *"...many legal immigrants from sub-Saharan Africa ...thanks to the carefully selected and passionately projected TV images of sub-Saharan African squalor and disease, are seen as toxic escapees of sub-humanity."*

I join other professionals in making a presentation
and the moment the event is over, one or two persons make it a point of duty to ask me: "How long
have you been here? Where did you learn to speak
English?" My responses vary. "My parents in Nigeria
speak good English." "I started speaking English as
a child in eastern Nigeria." "I used to teach English
and Business Communication in Republic of The
Gambia." "English is the lingua franca of Nigeria."

Chapter Six: Geo-branding shock and awe

"English is the language of instruction in Nigeria and I had my primary, secondary, polytechnic and university education there." "I edited a daily English newspaper in Republic of The Gambia."

My interviewers are shocked. They cannot imagine that I was very fluent in English many years before immigrating to the US. Because my accent points to my sub-continent of extraction, they conclude I must have undergone the popular English as a Second Language course in Iowa, which is not a bad thing though.

But they are not alone. Most people in post-industrialized nations do not know that English is widely spoken in Nigeria and Ghana just as French is widely spoken in Ivory Coast and Senegal. A lady asked me in Adelaide Australia if Africans still lived in trees, to which I sarcastically replied, "I know they wear trendy dresses."

The world simply likes to parade its ignorance of Africa as a badge of distinction probably because Poverty, Instability, Disease, Illiteracy and Corruption (PIDIC) which readily come to mind when Africa is mentioned also provides a make-me-feel-better massage for such inexcusable ignorance.

> "The world simply likes to parade its ignorance of Africa as a badge of distinction probably because Poverty, Instability, Disease, Illiteracy and Corruption (PIDIC) which readily come to mind when Africa is mentioned also provides a make-me-feel-better massage for such inexcusable ignorance."

I am sure if any of the aforementioned persons were a manufacturer of trendy clothes or an export management consultant, they would not imagine finding any buyer in Nigeria. Well, many of my relatives and friends in Nigeria wear trendy clothes, and some of them may be more comfortable and cash-loaded than many people I have seen in other parts of the world I have visited.

Ready buyer, unready sellers

Now, think of this other scenario. Someone with a Nigerian accent calls a real estate agent for a house on the market and the real estate agent says "It's sold." Then, someone with an Irish accent calls the same real estate agent who hastily asks, "When would you like to see the lovely property?" Is that double standard or what?

In August 2007, I called a Chicago car dealer seeking more information on a car I had seen on the Internet. A courteous female phone operator readily transferred me to a male car salesman who told me the car was available. He was very eager to sell the car immediately, perhaps to make much-needed commission on it but there was a problem. I was asking necessary follow-up questions about the car which he believed I shouldn't ask because my accent had suggested to him I was dumb. So, he angrily shouted, "Go take a rope and hang yourself" and banged the phone on me.

> *"I was asking necessary follow-up questions about the car which he believed I shouldn't ask because my accent had suggested to him I was dumb. So, he angrily shouted, "Go take a rope and hang yourself" and banged the phone on me"*

Upset and disappointed as I should be, I called the same number again to complain to a man who appeared to be a supervisor and he apologized but wasted no time in telling me the car his angry and apparently racist colleague had told me about 5 minutes ago was available for purchase had long been sold. In other words, the used car, as affordable as it was, was not meant for someone like me with an unmistakable foreign accent. At least, that's how I saw it.

I remember calling a Missouri-based car dealer sometime in 2007 to **BUY** some Honda and Toyota cars for export. I had told him I was ready to pay by wire transfer or by cashier's check upon receipt of his faxed invoice with the agreed prices. To my shock and dismay, he kept reiterating "You have to earn my confidence…You have to earn my confidence" just because I had told him I was a Nigerian living in the US. The last time I checked, it is the seller who should earn the confidence of the buyer, not the other way round. However, the rule changes if the buyer is a Nigerian (or any other African nationality) living in the US.

Apparently, the Missouri car dealer had concluded a Nigerian like me could not afford the cars in question. He must have thought of me as a helpless refugee or seen me through the blurred lens of recurring demeaning cable news images of hunger-stricken scavengers in Lagos or Nairobi.

Would he unleash that arguable racist rant on a Chinese, Canadian, Japanese or Portuguese-sounding prospect? I really, really doubt it.

I can go on and relate my ugly experiences in my daily interactions with other members of the common stock of humanity. In the evening of September 7, 2007, I boarded a flight from Seattle to Phoenix. A White couple repeatedly told me they didn't want me to sit beside them even though my boarding pass had said I should do so. The man and his wife told me to move somewhere else, and I had to, believing if I had insisted on maintaining my duly allocated seat, I would have been hastened to jail and charged with disturbing the peace. I changed flights a couple of times on that trip and had sat beside White people.

> **"A White couple repeatedly told me they didn't want me to sit beside them even though my boarding pass had said I should do so."**

On innumerable occasions when I called some used Mack truck sellers to make thousands of dollars worth of purchases, I got cold treatment owing to my ever present distinctive accent. But get this: The cold treatment always amazingly evaporated when my wife called with her American accent.

One day in 2007, I called a Toronto car company inquiring about the super cabs they advertised on their site. "They are sold," hurried a harsh male voice and the phone went dead. Then, my wife called and everything changed. There was courtesy. There were helpful details. There was communication. In fact, you would think the car salesman on the other side had been doing car business with my wife for many years. And I must note that she has received a couple of phone calls from that same company since then all because she wasn't me.

Still on double standards, if an international panel discussion on racism, globalization and militarism convenes in Detroit or Washington DC with a Chinese, an Australian, an American, a Mexican and a Nigerian as discussants, you can be sure of one thing: The Chinese would be introduced as Chinese, the Australian as Australian, the American as an American, the Mexican as Mexican, and you guessed right, the Nigerian as an African.

Chapter Six: Geo-branding shock and awe

Only people from African countries – especially Black African countries like Nigeria, Kenya, Democratic Republic of Congo, Ghana, Liberia, Sierra Leone, Mali, Namibia, Ivory Coast and Gambia – deserve to be introduced or described by their continental identity as Africans just as only poverty-stricken rural dwellers in some African countries deserve to be pitiable objects of media-driven NGO and celebrity events and fundraisers.

Is it didactic? Yes, of course! Shameful? You decide!

Being a life-long learner who believes a lot in cross-pollination of ideas and in event networking, I attend a lot of thematic socio-economic events in different parts of the world, and in many cases, especially in the Northern Hemisphere, it is a norm for even the most informed persons to introduce me as an African, instead of a Nigerian.

Such introduction which placates my national identity speaks real volumes of the low premium many people around the world place on Africa and Africans which is the major reason they treat Africa, a continent of 54 countries and about 740 million people, as a country.

Some have blamed it on "western" ignorance of Africa's geopolitical reality, which I believe must have informed the University of Iowa's "Africa is not a country" workshop.

> *"But the task of creating much-needed awareness and changing the negative perception of African countries in America is that of the citizens and governments of African countries and should be done in a way that will encourage Americans to invite Nigerian or Kenyan-made goods into their lives."*

But the task of creating much-needed awareness and changing the negative perception of African countries in America is that of the citizens and governments of African countries and should be done in a way that will encourage Americans to invite Nigerian or Kenyan-made goods into their lives.

There's ready help in an unexpected place

Nigeria, the country of Harvard-educated World Bank managing director Ngozi Okonjo-Iweala and

Chapter Six: Geo-branding shock and awe

US-based Philip Emeagwali, the supercomputer programmer and winner of the International Gordon Bell Prize in computer science, won its third Under-17 Soccer World Cup on Sunday, September 9 2007, and Americans are oblivious of it.

Did I hear you ask: Why should they care? After all, gas prices have gone up, Americans obviously find it hard to associate anything about computers with Nigeria, and soccer is not the sport of choice in America.

Yes, it isn't! But tickets for matches of the rebranded Los Angeles Galaxy which boasts British soccer superstar David Beckham have been selling out quickly, with all the attendant media frenzy that TV, radio, newspaper and Internet audiences know too well.

The Los Angeles Times reported in August 2007 that "Soccer merchandise and tickets have been sold in record numbers, not only here but in every MLS city, based on Beckham playing." **(1)**

What that tells me is that there is a yawning net of opportunity, a beckoning point of convergence for Nigeria and the US. A friendly match between Nigeria's World Cup champions, the Flying Eaglets, and the Los Angeles Galaxy would be a win-win for Nigeria and the US which is trying to make soccer a favorite US sport.

Thus, American sports entrepreneurs will make more money while at the same time promoting soccer that has produced such legends as Brazil's Pele and Nigeria's Kanu Nwankwo. Beckham-obsessed Americans (who greatly love celebrities) will find practical reasons to replace the Nigeria they associate with the strategically overblown advance fee fraud with the Nigeria that has one of the many things they want to have - soccer – which is a triumph of sports diplomacy.

In other words, soccer could be the perfect foot-in-the-door, eventually opening their hearts and eyes to **Nigeria's sterling tourist attractions from Rogeny Tourist Village, Yankari Game Reserve, Oguta Lake Resort with hotel and 18 hole golf course, Argungu Fishing and Cultural Festival and Obudu Cattle Ranch to Gurara Falls, Akassa Slave transit hall, Ibadan University Zoo, the nearly 1000-year-old Katsina Wall, the Iron of Liberty and the Mambilla Plateau.**

It could be a brave issuer of the much-needed arrest warrant for the media-driven Africa-is-good-for-nothing image that has been robbing Americans of the benefits of affordable but high quality Made-in-Nigeria goods like household furniture, clothing, and processed and unprocessed foods.
But that's if Nigeria emulates China in acting like a customer-driven corporate brand.

Chapter Seven

What "communist" China taught us

C hina readily comes to mind when affordable consumer products are mentioned
not just in America but also in Nigeria,
Canada, Australia and other countries of the world.
"China's reach,' as one source opined, 'now extends
from the Australian desert through the Sahara to the
Amazonian jungle" **(1)** trading their way to global
power with competitive goods and without war.**(2)**

Though it boasts a huge population of over a billion
people, its brand value is not in its population but in
its huge exports of innumerable products. China
manufactures and exports all imaginable kinds of
affordable household, office and sports products. It
is, for instance, the world's number one exporter of
toys, exporting over 22 billion toys in 2006, though
many of such toys were recalled in countries like the

US and Australia for unhealthy lead content. "China has gone from the United States' 18th to its 3rd largest trading partner," with bilateral trade moving from $8 billion in 1986 to $300 billion in 2006. **(3)**

The US reportedly had a trade deficit with China of about $232 billion in 2006 alone, which represents about 28% of US trade deficit that year. In late 2007, China's state-owned oil firm, Petrochina, became the world's first 1 trillion dollar company in what many experts believed was a great show of investor confidence in the world's fastest growing jumbo economy. Others however claimed the market value was simply too high and an offshoot of speculation. At $1 trillion, Petrochina has about twice the market value of US Exxon Mobil Corporation at $518 billion and General Electric at $420 billion.

Yes, "communist" China became China the Great!

Whether China will sustain its bull market and amazing economic boom is certainly another issue, but such economic boom did not happen overnight. China has been making itself ready for it through a host of deliberate economic policies, growth-geared actions and events which include (in no order of importance):

- economic reforms introduced and championed by Deng Xiaoping in 1978;
- the appeal and power of Chinese all-you-can-eat restaurants around the world;
- the popularity of Chinese movies which remarkably showcase China;
- the robust export facilitation role played by Chinese nationals who currently live or had lived in America and other countries;
- the ubiquity of the carefully informing and clearly educating China Central Television (CCTV9) I watch frequently in Iowa;
- the **One Village, One Product** initiative – also working in Japan and Thailand – that is helping to significantly boost local productivity, entrepreneurship and livelihoods;
- the glaring power of global e-commerce websites like Alibaba.com and Ecvv.com which make it easy to discover, appreciate and contact many Chinese manufacturers and suppliers;
- China's triumphant admission into the World Trade Organization (WTO) on December 11 2001;
- the seeming global appeal and penetration of Chinese martial arts seen through the value lens of health, fitness and soccer mom esteem; and
- China's Permanent Normal Trade Relations (PNTR) status which gave Chinese goods

permanent, unlimited and unconditional access to the huge US market.

These happened over a period of three decades, propelled by clear vision and vigor amid arguably inevitable bumps and blisters.

> *"China ...is now re-tooling its healthy image as the world's factory to a healthier one as a "true innovator" especially with its new hydrogen-powered car with zero emission - a 100 per cent green vehicle that promises to sell very well in this era of star-studded campaigns on global warming and the resultant public awareness and concern."*

Yet, China in its methodical embrace and adaptive application of market economy appears determinedly pursuant of greater economic significance and clout around the world. It is now re-tooling its healthy image as the world's factory and **engine room of retail diplomacy** to a healthier one as a "true innovator" especially with its new hydrogen-powered car with zero emission - a 100 per cent green vehicle that

promises to sell very well in this era of star-studded
campaigns on global warming and the resultant public awareness and concern. According to CCTV9,
"In many countries, green vehicles may be just a
concept. In China, however, they're ready to make
their debut during the 2008 Olympic Games." **(4)**

Little wonder then that when Chinese president Hu
Jintao visited the US in April 2006, his first port of
call wasn't Washington DC - as would a Brand Africa president - but Seattle in the trade-driven Washington State where he met with Microsoft's Bill
Gates and other corporate heavy weights before going to meet with President Bush in Washington DC.
By so doing, President Jintao clearly underscored
where China's interest in the US was – international
trade and investments, not the photo-op diplomacy
that leaders of African nations like Nigeria place the
highest premium on, and hire surface-scratching
Washington DC lobbyists to facilitate.

> *"President Jintao clearly underscored
> where China's interest in the US was –
> international trade and investments, not
> the photo-op diplomacy that leaders of
> African nations like Nigeria place the
> highest premium on, and hire surface-
> scratching Washington DC lobbyists to
> facilitate."*

For China, it wasn't so much about Japanese-like product quality as it was about export quantity and product affordability, knowing that there are billions of people around the world who for obvious reasons care more about quantity and affordability than quality. China's was a clearly targeted multi-product diplomacy which undoubtedly helped it increase its number of billionaires from 15 in 2006 to 106 in 2007. This, according to one news report, "underlined the rapidly growing economic muscle of the Asian giant." **(5)**

But can you imagine that nearly four decades ago, China was a no-go area to many American companies in need of dependable suppliers of large quantities of assorted products? China was seen as lacking the industrial and distribution capacity to deliver good quality products. It was such that in President Nixon's groundbreaking presidential visit to China in 1972, economic and trade issues were subordinated to diplomatic and security issues, according to a report by the US Chamber of Commerce. **(6)**

Care for my opinion? I think it had to do with China's American boardroom, ballroom and bedroom image as a communist nation, which I don't think it was – and I know you would be surprised to read that. But I will go on and proffer a brief explanation of the difference between communism and socialism and then bring in the 1989 collapse of socialism in Poland and the eventual collapse of USSR in 1991 to, among other things, (A) highlight an important strategic lesson that China learnt, and (B) underscore why the Brand Africa misnomer should collapse like USSR, thus allowing Nigeria, for instance, to rise up and live up to its Goldman Sachs ranking among the **Next 11 (N-11) countries.**

By Marxist standards, China, at best, was and still is a socialist country tempered by market economy, just like Russia, because it has large stock piles of arms and other instruments of coercion and cohesion like the police and the judiciary. While such instruments could be used in a socialist transition period precipitated by a proletarian revolution that overthrew the oppressive bourgeois class, they could not be used afterwards. The transition period then serves to completely eliminate all the vestiges of the bourgeois class, all the instruments it uses to oppress and suppress the working class.

Communism thus emerges out of that process as the state "withers away". But, in real terms, communism has never emerged anywhere. There has been no "stateless" and "classless" society anywhere that I know. Thus, when you hear of the Communist Party of China or the South African Communist Party, the sentiment is of what should be, not what is. Communism has proven to be a mental construct, a stupendous utopia. It has never seen the light of day and will never see the light of day because no society can practically operate on Karl Marx' 1875 dictum of

"From each according to his ability, to each according to his need." **(7)** None! It sounds very appealing to the poor and the weak but not to the rich and powerful because of the obvious risk factors to them.

> *"I am often baffled when people conclude that the dreaded USSR (Union of Soviet Socialist Republics) collapsed because President Ronald Reagan went to West Berlin on June 12, 1987 and simply said, "Mr. Gorbachev, tear down this wall.""*

Chinese people describe theirs as socialism, not communism even though the ruling party is called the Communist Party of China and the country is glaringly a quasi market economy. While keynoting the 17th national congress of the party on October 15, 2007, Chinese president Hu Jintao called on the Chinese people to hold high the **"great banner of socialism with Chinese characteristics,"** stressing the need for sustainable growth and greater democracy.

USSR collapses, China learns

I am often baffled when people conclude that the
dreaded USSR (Union of Soviet Socialist Republics)
collapsed because President Ronald Reagan went to
West Berlin on June 12, 1987 and simply said, "Mr.
Gorbachev, tear down this wall." **(8)** I know the ut-
terances of American presidents are powerful but in
this case, those of beloved President Reagan did not
go as far as bringing down the anathema Berlin Wall.

Five major things led to the collapse of mighty
USSR, proffering lessons to China:

(A) Northern powers (often called the west) reinvented or better put, re-branded capitalism, fine
tuning its image of Social Darwinism (survival of the
fittest) with a strictly instrumentalist, faceless view of
workers to that which strongly protects the wealth of
the owner of the means of production and distribution while giving opportunities and deserved benefits
to the workers. Remember George W. Bush's "compassionate conservatism" that sought to re-brand the
Republican Party after its eight-year absence in the
White House? It can help you understand what happened to capitalism and why. Capitalism was re-
branded and made to look compassionate and more
appealing to those who would ordinarily prefer socialism.

Thus, there came improved working conditions (better wages and appreciable fringe benefits) which made workers happier, capitalism look better and the wealth of the rich more secure. How did this necessary re-branding come about? Though Prussia had come up with a compulsory health insurance law by 1854, many still see German Chancellor Otto von Bismarck as the father of this capitalist re-branding that made socialism lose much of its worker-centric appeal. Bismarck in 1883 successfully masterminded the compulsory health insurance law, financed by state subsidies. Its success inspired the spread of health insurance and worker protection programs across Europe.

It is worthy of note here that Karl Marx and his associate, Friedrich Engels, with whom he wrote the incisive *The Communist Manifesto* in 1848, were Germans. The National Health Service (NHS) emerged in Britain in 1948 (which was preceded by the 1911 Insurance Act). But before Britain's NHS, there was the depression-stirred Social Security Act of 1935 in the US, which, at that time, did not receive a groundswell of reception as many had thought it was something the US government had devised to interfere in their personal lives.

(B) The good work of UN agencies like UNICEF, FAO, WHO and UNESCO greatly complimented the efforts of northern nations like America, Britain and Germany as illuminated above, thus significantly reducing the appeal of socialism to workers and the poor, especially in developing nations of the south.

(C) The USSR expansionist incursion into Afghanistan proved suicidal. It was hugely costly in terms of money (as it had wasted about $57 billion), materials and national humiliation because by the time it finally pulled out of Afghanistan in February 1989, it was clearly demythologized and weakened economically, ideologically and militarily. Life became unbearable for its citizens most of whom had to queue for long hours for basic needs like milk and meat amid high and excruciating unemployment. There came a wind of factory closures, empty shops, and commonplace despair that stimulated a natural popular desire for better life and change.

(D) The glaring gulf between living standards in socialist Eastern Germany and capitalist Western Germany – the former low, the latter high – made great case for capitalism. Both were separated not only by the now-extinct Berlin Wall but also by the ideologies of socialism and capitalism. And when people in Eastern Germany saw that life was livelier and better in Western Germany than in their country and found palpable reasons to blame it on their country's socialist thrust, they yearned for capitalism, they clamored to be like people on the other side of the Berlin Wall. When they could not take it any longer, when they had had enough of the comparatively poor living conditions, they went for the Wall and brought it down. And in doing so, they also broke the back of the USSR, which lost its very strategic satellite state.

(E) The knock out punch of the "failed" August 1991 coup involving Valentin Varennikov and others who saw reformist Soviet leader Mikhail Gorbachev (riding on his glasnost and perestroika) as a traitor and destructive agent of the global oil industry mafia. Thus, by December 1991, the Belovezhskaya Pushcha accords that say "The USSR ceases its existence as a subject of international law and a geopolitical reality" had become glaringly inevitable. Gorbachev formally resigned on December 25 and the once mighty USSR became history.

> *"Positive change is not a bestowed gift but a hard earned wage."*

So, what is my point? Positive change is not a bestowed gift but a hard earned wage. As far as I know, President Ronald Reagan probably did as much as Pope John Paul, a native of Poland, where the revolt against socialism and USSR influence entered the fast lane, although many give the Pope little credit. But the Pope had started as early as 1979 with his home-pilgrimage, sparking off a serene re-awakening of the Polish sense of identity, history and self-consciousness which energized the Lech Walesa-led Polish labor movement, the Solidarity. That movement eventually toppled the socialist regime of Poland and set the much-needed example for others across the Soviet bloc.

Lech Walesa himself had attributed their victory to the inspiration they got from Pope John Paul, saying "The pope started this chain of events that led to the end of communism".(9) The last Soviet leader, Mikhail Sergeyevich Gorbachev, agreed, saying: "What has happened in Eastern Europe in recent years would not have been possible without the presence of this Pope, without the great role even political that he has played on the world scene." (10)

The events in Poland obviously emboldened people in other countries in the Soviet bloc as regimes in East Germany, Czechoslovakia, Hungary, Bulgaria and Romania started falling one after the other. Romanians even had to execute their head of state in utter disgust.

So, suffice it to say that change such as the one that took place in Poland in 1989 and the one that should take place with Brand Africa don't just happen. It happens because visionaries, inspirers and action-driven people rise up to the challenges of their time. What if African countries like Nigeria could enlist the help of a world renowned inspirational patriot like Pope John Paul and a pragmatic icon like Lech

Walesa in tackling the image problem that seriously affects its trade and tourism?

> *"The chain of events that radically transformed China's status in world trade didn't fall from trees. The transformation happened because China was alive to its tough challenges..."*

The chain of events that radically transformed China's status in world trade didn't fall from trees. The transformation happened because China was alive to its tough challenges, tapping into the knowledge, consciousness, diligence and aspirations of its people to effectively re-brand itself.

Yet, I must clarify here that I am not a China apologist. Nor am I recommending socialism let alone communism. I am only using the foregoing analysis to show how the then Brand China associated with "communism" adversely affected its trade especially in countries like America just as today's Brand Africa associated with Poverty, Instability, Disease, Illiteracy and Corruption (PIDIC) is adversely affecting America's trade and tourism relations with countries like Nigeria, South Africa, Kenya and Ethiopia. Didactically, China acted, and did so methodically, consistently and purposefully.

I believe China learnt a lot from (A) the re-branding of capitalism, and (B) the demise of USSR which I highlighted above.

But what specifically did China do?

It realized it could not win in the capitalism-socialism debate. It came home to the truism that Americans, like the British, Canadians and Australians, will never be favorably disposed to the dreaded "communism"; that as long as it had the scary label of "communist" China in American media, its manufacturers and distributors will not be doing big business with America.

So, it decided not to repair but to replace the "communist China Brand" that was anathema in the North especially America while still embracing its own version of socialism. It brilliantly re-branded itself, projecting something its target markets in the North are happy with - the **Made-in-China Brand**. But unlike Japan (which had a negative image in the US as a result of World War 11) that successfully built three global brands, Toyota, Honda and Sony, their best global diplomats, China's brand, in keeping with the ubiquitous all-you-can-eat Chinese restaurants many Americans love, became an all-goods-you-can-buy affair. It manufactured very plenty and the world bought very plenty as well.

> *"China's brand, in keeping with the ubiquitous all-you-can-eat Chinese restaurants many Americans love, became an all-goods-you-can-buy affair. It manufactured very plenty and the world bought very plenty as well. "*

This is the triumph of multi-product diplomacy or lifestyle diplomacy that has not only helped in giving China the world's largest foreign reserves of $1.2 trillion but also a very significant influence over suspect regimes in Myanmar, Iran, North Korea and Sudan that understandably worries America and its allies.

Such triumph of **lifestyle diplomacy** is also very evident in the fact that Americans now sleep in Chinese-made clothes on Chinese-made bedspreads under Chinese-made fans after watching sensational cable news on Chinese-made big screen TV sets and eating dinner made with Chinese-made spices and served with Chinese-made dinner bowls or conveniently at nearby all-you-can-eat Chinese restaurants. So, where is "communism" or the fear of it in all that? Nowhere! Can you see how misunderstanding-propelled fear develops wings and flies and unpleasant images get bleach therapy?

Worthy of note here is the fact that China did not say, "The unwelcome "communist" China Brand is an Asian problem. So, let's deal with it collectively as Asians," as African nations like Nigeria do. Rather, it saw it as a national problem, a Chinese problem, and while it may have collaborated with other Asian nations along the way, it solved the "communist" China Brand problem as China, not as Asia.

It is also worthy of note that China came to the US and created both the need and the outlets for their products. Their popular all-you-can-eat restaurants and Chinese movies featuring the likes of Jacky Chan and Jet Li made Americans (and citizens of other nations like Britain and Australia) not only at ease with China but also to like China and its people. The restaurants and movies were the foot-in-the-door for China, the John the Baptist of their all-goods-you-can-buy diplomacy. Then came the ubiquitous and popular dollar stores and, of course, the mighty and undoubtedly ubiquitous Wal-Mart that became great outlets for innumerable assortments of affordable Chinese products.

Other nations do likewise, creating the need and outlets for their signature products. Though Toyota,
Honda and Sony are well known Japanese brands,
the brand owners are in America in full force, pushing the reach, value and patronage of their brands.

> **"China came to the US and created both
> the need and the outlets for their
> products."**

So, what am I recommending to African nations like
Nigeria? They should carefully and directly introduce
relevant products into the American lifestyle. The
era of waiting for people in target markets like
America to wake up one morning and just feel like
visiting Nigeria to buy its export products and services or to enjoy its remarkable tourist attractions is
gone, and people in other parts of the world like the
Chinese know it. The world has changed, and so
have ways of promoting and facilitating trade and
tourism.

For instance, there are American universities today
that urge people in their target audiences not to go
to college but to let college come to them in the
form of distance education. They attract a lot of

busy working professionals who can access their Internet classrooms from the comfort of their homes and offices or even at coffee shops and gyms.

Nigerians make good quality clothes and shoes but China is very big on clothes and shoes and it would be very difficult to displace China in a market where it has strong global dominance. Nigerians also process foods but because of Nigeria's PIDIC image, people in America would not be favorably disposed to Nigerian processed foods. They will certainly have many quality concerns – hygiene, preservation, etc. But Nigerians make beautiful household and office furniture that can compete with furniture anywhere.

A Nigerian furniture chain starting off with five strategically located stores in Atlanta, Chicago, New York, Seattle and Detroit with both ready-to-go and customized orders will make many Americans to begin to see Nigeria through the appreciative and deserving lens of beautiful, durable and affordable Nigerian furniture, instead of the carefully shot and projected images of refuse heaps they see on their big TV screens.

Chapter Eight

Dismantling Brand Africa

"**F**lowers from Rwanda, music from Mali, clothing from Mauritius, outsourcing services from Ghana: these are among the diverse successes of African entrepreneurs determined to make globalization work for them, their families, and their communities" **(1)** was how a World Bank official opened his widely published op-ed on export challenges facing African countries.

Such information on non-oil and mining exports must be profoundly amazing to many in America who could hardly imagine consumer product exports from those countries – all because of Brand Africa. And though the remaining 50 African countries also have many other export products and services, the continent's share of the world total has been very low, decreasing from 6.3% in 1980 to 2.5% in 2004 and 2% in 2006 due mainly, in my opinion, to Brand Africa.

> *"Brand Africa has been Guantanamo Bay to 54 nation brands that need the fresh air and liberty of re-branding. It should therefore give way to re-invented Brand Nigeria, Brand South Africa and Brand Kenya (and so on)"*

I strongly believe Brand Africa which lumps and limits 54 African nations together, seeing them through the blurred lens of Poverty, Instability, Disease, Illiteracy and Corruption (PIDIC), has never worked and will never work in the interest of any of the 54 African countries. Brand Africa has been Guantanamo Bay to 54 nation brands that need the fresh air and liberty of re-branding. It should therefore be radically replaced with repackaged and replenished Brand Nigeria, Brand South Africa, Brand Gambia, Brand Kenya and so on that can be taken seriously in target markets like America when international tourism and global trade come to mind.

Reformed markets like Mauritius, Botswana, Ghana and Nigeria – though completely without global consumer brands – not only produce consumer products but also boast remarkable tourist attractions that can keep tourists coming back again and again but they are scared of Brand Africa that is understood as synonymous with insecurity and insignificance. That Brand Africa construct also ensures that many American businesses ignore AGOA, the African Growth and Opportunity Act, because they do not associate eligible countries like Nigeria, Kenya and Ethiopia with quality consumer products.

> *"Brand Africa has been a besieged crowd of 54 countries latching unto one another partly emotionally and partly economically without demonstrating their distinguishable and compelling attributes needed to significantly impact the world."*

Let's look at an analogy here. Rock and rap are not my favorites but they are very popular music genres especially among certain segments of the US population. But have you ever wondered what could happen if a 54-member rock or rap band emerges on the scene? I sincerely don't think it would be fun or trend setting because 54 is so huge a crowd for a rock or rap band.

Again, if you are on a hospital bed and you are surrounded by 54 doctors, I am sure you won't be comfortable. Would you? How can you know which one is your real doctor? There are so many of them perhaps expressing their differing medical opinions verbally or non-verbally at the same time, and that could be very unsettling.

In the same vein, Brand Africa has been a besieged crowd of 54 countries latching unto one another partly emotionally and partly economically without demonstrating their distinguishable and compelling attributes needed to significantly impact the world.

South Africa, a G20 country, apparently understands this, which is why, though a strong member of the Africa Union and the New Partnership for Africa's Development (NEPAD), it is vigorously promoting South-South trade with India and Brazil under the annual India-Brazil-South Africa (IBSA) summit.

But exports of mainly raw materials from sub-Saharan African countries like Nigeria and South Africa to Asian countries like China and India have been recording significant increase in the last decade **not** because sub-Saharan African countries have been in much-needed vibrant export marketing mode but because their raw materials are desperately

needed for the development of these Asian economies - which go for what they need – just as they
have been for Europe and America.

Standing with arms akimbo and expecting transmog-
rification of the international system is not an option. The initiative to reverse the trend must come
from these sub-Saharan African countries many of
which are now **reformed markets**. And it requires a
common sense practical approach like China's, especially in pleading their own cause themselves.

For instance, just as Hollywood movies and cable
networks like CNN have contributed very greatly in
promoting Brand America around the world, including African countries like Nigeria, Nigeria's Nollywood movie industry said to be the third largest in
the world should also contribute very greatly in
promoting Nigeria's image and its products and services as well as attracting lots of tourists from the
northern hemisphere. How? By going mainstream in
America like Chinese movies. Think of what could
happen when well produced and marketed Nollywood movies feature well known American celebrities and become available in American theaters and
on the shelves of Wal-Mart, Target and Walgreen's.

Also, think of what could happen when one of the
moneybags in Nigeria launches a Nigeria-focused
international TV network available 24-7 around the
world like China's CCTV9 and offered in America

through well known providers like Dish Network. Won't it make a great difference like CCTV9? I found CCTV9 on Dish Network a couple of years ago while browsing the channels, and I have since then continued to watch it for information on China and other Asian markets.

The fact remains that without media attention, there is no branding or re-branding. Without effectively getting the right word out, there is no personal, corporate or nation brand. Branding, like wedding cake, is baked in the media and cut in applauded sales.

> *"Branding, like wedding cake, is baked in the media and cut in applauded sales."*

So, with avenues like mainstream Nollywood movies and Nigeria-focused TV news network available 24-7 around the world especially in target export markets, the world would finally learn of great but hitherto suppressed trade, tourism and investment opportunities in Nigeria, and other African countries. The World Bank in a release it issued on April 7 2003 revealed that "The rate of return on FDI was highest in sub-Saharan Africa, compared with other regions in the world," **(2)** a view shared by US government's Overseas Private Investment Corporation. Why then does it attract least investments? I am glad you asked, and here is my simple answer: Brand Africa. Africa's PIDIC image scares investors except, of course, those in need of raw materials like oil, natural gas, coffee, cocoa, diamond, gold, uranium, cobalt and coltan (used in making your cell phones, computers, DVD players) as well as chromium, platinum, and a host of others.

Do many Americans know the sleek cell phones they use owe a lot to the Democratic Republic of Congo that was embroiled in a long coltan-driven war that claimed many lives and displaced many more? No! "Research by International Peace Information Service, an independent Belgian institute, shows that European companies trading coltan
in the Democratic Republic of the Congo contribute to the financing of the Congolese war," reports The Namibian. **(3)** Americans know cell phone brands like Nokia, Samsung, Motorola and Sony Ericsson, not where the raw materials that make cell phones are sourced.

Brand Africa confines Africa to raw materials

Brand Africa has served to pigeon-hole sub-Saharan Africa as supplier of raw materials and cheap labor for the development of other parts of the world. When European powers like Britain, Germany, France and Belgium needed raw materials and cheap labor to develop, they turned to sub-Saharan Africa. When the US needed cheap labor for its development, it turned to sub-Saharan Africa, mostly kidnapping and at times buying able bodied men and women – which is why we have about 40 million African-Americans today.

> *"China...has unsurprisingly turned to sub-Saharan Africa ...for raw materials like oil, copper and gold even if it meant propping up the genocidal regime of Omar Hassan al-Bashir in Khartoum."*

Now that China is walking super fast on the lane of industrial development and global mega influence, it has unsurprisingly turned to sub-Saharan Africa too, cutting deals left, right and center with countries therein for raw materials like oil, copper and gold even if it meant propping up the genocidal regime of Omar Hassan al-Bashir in Khartoum. While people of conscience around the world condemn the genocide in Darfur by the Khartoum government-sponsored Janjaweed militias, they tend to lose sight of the vital fact that **China is practically funding the operations, standing tall as its leading supplier of weapons of war, buying 60% of Sudan's oil and owning as much as 40% of its Greater Nile Petroleum Operating Co. (4)**

Africa has been branded for centuries as good only for raw materials and cheap labor, which is why though Nigeria is the fifth largest oil supplier to the US, and many Nigerian professionals like medical doctors, software engineers, journalists, nurses, pharmacists and professors are working across America, Nigeria is not visible in American boardrooms, ballrooms and bedrooms. An average American is very unlikely to imagine that Nigeria has anything to do with the gas they buy at the pumps or the educational and health sectors of America. After all, the Brand Africa they know through the media is all about Poverty, Instability, Disease, Illiteracy and Corruption (PIDIC).

Ivory Coast is the world's largest producer of cocoa but how many Americans and Canadians can draw the connection between the African country of Ivory

Coast and the Hershey, Mars or Nestle chocolate brands they love to have as daytime snacks or desserts? Very few, I believe! The same is also true of the connection between the ubiquitous Starbucks brand they love so much and the premium coffee of Ethiopia, Africa's largest producer of coffee. When coffee is mentioned, they think of Starbucks, the leading brand, and rightly so because Starbucks coffee is easily within reach and ready-to-gulp. It is a very popular lifestyle, but unlike Ethiopian coffee farmers, Starbucks is making lots of money.

My point is that being only a source of raw materials and cheap labor for industrialized nations has not been and will never be rewarding for African countries because it perpetuates Brand Africa. Since sub-Saharan African countries like Nigeria and South Africa actually manufacture good quality but little known consumer products at a time post-industrial nations like America have become service economies (banking, insurance, travel, media, etc) and thus turn elsewhere for needed consumer products, carefully launched and sustained consumer product diplomacy - which I also call lifestyle diplomacy - would greatly change the PIDIC image I have elaborated on in many parts of this book.

Thus, Nigerian consumer products will make Nigeria visible to American consumers who invite Nigeria into their boardrooms, ballrooms and bedrooms, accomplishing what photo-op, rotunda and black-tie dinner diplomacy could not accomplish in Washington DC for decades.

"Nigerian consumer products will make Nigeria visible to American consumers who invite Nigeria into their boardrooms, ballrooms and bedrooms, accomplishing what photo-op, rotunda and black-tie dinner diplomacy could not accomplish in Washington DC for decades."

Why am I so confident?

A recent World Bank report acknowledges that "for the first time in three decades, African economies are growing with the rest of the world. Average growth in the Sub-Saharan economies was 5.4 percent in 2005 and 2006. The consensus projection is 5.3 percent for 2007 and 5.4 percent for 2008." **(5)**

The report went on to posit that:

A. Policies in many sub-Saharan African countries have been getting better;
B. Many sub-Saharan African economies are more open to trade and private enterprise;
C. Many sub-Saharan African countries have better governance and more assaults on corruption;
D. Many sub-Saharan African countries have more manageable foreign debt payments, inflation, budget deficits and exchange rates.

Isn't that reassuring, coming from the Bretton Woods system?

Many African countries like South Africa and Nigeria have never been as product export and foreign direct investment (FDI) ready as they are today though more needs to be done. Many are beginning to invest increasingly in research and development (R&D), many are beginning to treat improvement of the skills of their work force as a major priority, many are responding in varying degrees to the blazing need to focus on their core competencies/comparative advantages, and to expand their target markets beyond industrialized nations like America where bad press, among other things, religiously limits them. Those are very good developments but more needs to be done.

Chapter Eight: Dismantling Brand Africa

On September 26 2007, The World Bank and the International Finance Corporation released the "Doing Business 2008" **(6)** report citing Mauritius as the easiest place to do business on the continent of Africa. That sets Mauritius apart but is Mauritius setting itself apart from Brand Africa. The same report also says Kenya and Ghana, two other African countries, are among the top 10 business reformers in the world.

So, you can see why lumping these countries together under Brand Africa has not brought (and will not bring) the aforementioned positive developments to light. But will this resonate with Africa-trashing Black immigrants, the elite wing of the American media, the China-obsessed American business community, and the American consumers that seem to prefer pity and prejudice-evoking Brand Africa? I believe they are waiting for Brand Mauritius, Brand Kenya and Brand Ghana to stand up to be counted as Brand China did.

A September 2007 survey by Mo Ibrahim and Professor Robert Rotberg of Harvard University rates Mauritius as the best governed country in sub-Saharan Africa, followed by Seychelles, Botswana, Cape Verde and South Africa. Others on the top 10 list are Gabon, Namibia, Ghana, Senegal, and São Tomé and Príncipe. **(7)** The survey is said to be "the world's most comprehensive ranking of African governance."**(8)**

Botswana, another African country, reportedly has A1/A2 credit ratings and is politically stable. But will this resonate with Africa-trashing Black immigrants, the elite wing of the American media, the China-obsessed American business community, and the American consumers that seem to prefer pity and prejudice-evoking Brand Africa? I believe they are waiting for Brand Botswana to stand up to be counted as Brand China did.

A 2007 report by the African Development Bank portrays South Africa, Algeria, Nigeria and Egypt (the SANE countries) as economic powerhouses on the continent. But will this resonate with Africa-trashing Black immigrants, the elite wing of the American media, the China-obsessed American business community, and the American consumers that seem to prefer pity and prejudice-evoking Brand Africa? I believe they are waiting for Brand Algeria, Brand Egypt, Brand Nigeria and Brand South Africa to stand up to be counted as Brand China did.

The British Broadcasting Corporation reported in July 2006 that "South Africa's 2010 football World Cup is set to be the most commercially successful since the first tournament was held 76 years ago," with FIFA president Sepp Blatter saying the contracts they had already signed for the event exceeded those they signed for the 2006 World Cup in Germany by 25%. **(9)** Can you believe it? The world football governing body got $821 million contracts for the South African event in 2010 compared to the $700 million they got for the one in 2006 in the BMW and Mercedes Benz country of Germany. Yet, many people in the Northern Hemisphere still see the African continent of my extraction as a heap of ruins, a place from where no good thing comes, a cap-in-hand village where most people run around half-naked with hunting spears.

But as the German brand gatekeeper and Fortune Magazine's most powerful woman of the world, Chancellor Angela Merkel, observed about preparations for the 2010 World Cup, "Billions of people around the world will look at what you created and it will become a global symbol of South Africa." **(10)**

In other words, Brand South Africa will become globally visible and will evoke positive sentiments around the world as a result of the global event. And that's what South Africa needs. Northern business media like CNBC that claims to be first in worldwide business news and analysis has shown it adjudges the Johannesburg Stock Exchange (JSE) unworthy of deserved frequent spotlight even as the rest of the big-players-only corporate media think of South Africa in terms of mine accidents and workers rescue because of Brand Africa.

The Brand Africa that has been vigorously promoted by big NGOS like Feed The Children, giant cable

TV networks like CNN, and world renown celebrities like Angelina Jolie, superstar Bono and most recently Paris Hilton may have yielded some well trumpeted handouts but has certainly not facilitated much-needed economic growth and development in sub-Saharan African countries from Nigeria to Namibia and should therefore be jettisoned.

This Brand Africa that has routinely evoked pity or prejudice, restraining or scaring average prospective investors, tourists and product importers instead of engendering trade and tourism has been like a drowsy and despised military junta leader blazingly deserving of the proper branding decision of indefatigable democracy-geared mass demonstrations.

Like full term pregnancy, Nigeria, Kenya, South Africa, Botswana, Ghana, Mauritius and other **reformed markets** in Africa should – in their fourth, fifth or sixth decade of nationhood - be hidden no more.

They should strive perspicaciously and persistently to scale the geo-branding barriers imposed on them by:

A. the better-than-thou Northern media which is quick, circumscribed and unrelenting in trumpeting natural and man-made tragedies in sub-Saharan African countries while directly and indirectly promoting products and

services of favorite Asian countries in dem-
onstration of inverted objectivity;

B. Africa-trashing Black immigrants (from Nigeria to Kenya) who have been breeding
generations of Blacks in the Diaspora with
gravely disturbing dissociation and disen-
chantment with their countries of origin in
Africa;

C. personal brand repositioning "Pity Africa"
celebrities who hide under raising awareness
about HIV/Aids, civil wars and poverty in
Africa to push, reposition or regenerate their
brands; and

D. masterful misery marketing global NGOs
operating in sub-Saharan African countries
who exploit very carefully selected images of
penurious living conditions for endless fundraising, with a large chunk of funds raised
diverted to sponsoring the lavish lifestyle of
some staff members in those African countries - and I am not writing here about what
I have heard but what I have seen.

By scaling the long-running barriers and applying the
many practical but by no means exhaustive ways I
have offered throughout the pages of this book, they
would be on their way to "Winning like China."

I believe sub-Saharan African countries, while heal-
ing their self-inflicted wounds of corruption and political greed, should accept the immutability of the

social Darwinistic thrust of the international system and muster the requisite wisdom and courage to painstakingly lift their quality consumer products and services up to strong and sustained global glare, appraisal and patronage.

Like the USSR that collapsed in 1991 for the nations of Russia, Armenia, Azerbaijan, Estonia, Georgia, Ukraine, Latvia, Uzbekistan, Kazakhstan and others to emerge, Brand Africa should be dismantled to make way for reinvented, refocused and repositioned Brand Nigeria, Brand South Africa, Brand Botswana, Brand Kenya, Brand Mauritius and others that are properly disseminated and "customer-driven."

Yes, this belated no-looking-back dismantling of Brand Africa should usher in a newfound country-specific thrust of **lifestyle diplomacy** that has worked for the once resented "communist" China, helping it to become the world's fourth largest economy, and for America's World War II foe Japan, helping it to become the world's second largest economy.

Conclusion

To enable you fully grasp the essence of this book explicitly and challengingly titled ***Don't Africa Me: 'Their' geo-branding war, 'Our' trade, tourism wounds, and Winning like China***, here are 13 major viewpoints of mine that run through its pages:

1. Africa is a continent of 54 countries with about 740 million inhabitants, not a country. For too long, these 54 countries have been lumped and limited together as Brand Africa seen rigidly through what I call the PIDIC (poverty, instability, disease, illiteracy and corruption) lens.

2. Since an American is not called a North American, a Nigerian, Gambian, Kenyan, South African or Ghanaian should not be called an African. Africa is a continent like

North America and Nigeria is a country like America. Calling a Nigerian an African while calling a Chinese a Chinese is not just unfair but derogatory.

3. The African continent is not as bad, helpless and hopeless as it is persistently portrayed by better-than-thou and powerful opportunists. No doubt, there are high incidences of corruption, diseases and poverty in African countries but every country in the world, including the US, has its own share of these despicable ailments. Besides, there are many good things happening in African countries that are deliberately ignored **to make those who ignore them feel better and superior.** There are good people, good products, good events and good tourist attractions in every African country, and I am talking about what I know, not what I read or heard.

4. African economies like Nigeria and South Africa which I call **reformed markets** are growing as fast or even faster – at 5.4% - than many countries in the North and are glowing in trade and investment opportunities which are not only known but also mined for gold by big corporations. Wondering who is left out in the process? Average citizens and small businesses in northern countries like America because they believe whatever the corporate media tells them about Africa.

5. Some African-Americans dissociate themselves from the continent of Africa for the obvious fact that many countries therein are not as globally visible or economically strong as the Asian countries of China, India, South Korea, Japan, Malaysia and Singapore. Thus, if Kenya is as visible in America as China seen through things like Chinese movies, ubiquitous all-you-can-eat restaurants, CCTV9, dollar stores and all-you-can-buy consumer products at Wal-Mart, and Ghana as visible as Japan seen through global brands like Honda and Toyota cars, those African Americans will sing a different tune. This is a simple human trait. People want to be where they think the action is and to many, "seeing is believing," which is why they identify with China and believe the carefully shot and projected TV images about Africa. African countries should therefore act in clear understanding of this trait as they seek to expand their trade and tourism and to attract more corporate and private foreign investments.

6. No doubt, big corporations shape media focus, policy thrust and public opinion in developed countries like America, Canada and United Kingdom. To big corporations in such developed countries, Africa's role in the global economy is and should remain that of source of raw materials for manufacturing.

In other words, as the Asian country of Japan is globally known for Toyota and Honda, the whole of Africa should be known in boardrooms for raw materials. On the other hand, the corporate media and global NGOs believe it should be known for poverty, instability, disease, illiteracy and corruption (PIDIC). Both views are not good for Africa.

7. Most buyers of consumer items do not know or care to know the source of raw materials used in making such items. They only identify with the brands making or selling them. Examples here are Exxon Mobil (oil), Starbucks (coffee) and Hershey (cocoa).

8. The better-than-thou corporate media, Black immigrants oblivious of present-day reform and growth across Africa, celebrities exploiting Africa to reposition their personal brands and expand their fortunes, and donations-worshipping global NGOs are leading the charge against African countries, constantly creating the impression that African countries are up to no good. **This turns people away and hurts trade, tourism and investments in African countries.**

9. Many highly skilled immigrants from African countries labor beyond measure to speak with American accent believing that speaking with such borrowed accent would make people they come across think they are Afri-

can-Americans, not people born on the continent of Africa. This shuts out their countries of origin.

10. The corporate media provides covering fire for big corporations as they exploit natural resources across Africa. How? They do so by creating and sustaining the impression that Africa is up to no good, so many individuals and small businesses in the North are not attracted to African countries because if they ever experience the real Africa, they will feel encouraged to blow the lid off the besieged continent.

11. African governments and private sector **ARE NOT** as proactive and aggressive as they should be in strategic marketing and brand management. There are many common sense ways African countries (governments, civil and corporate citizens) can win the geo-branding war against them, and they are found on many pages of *Don't Africa Me.* African governments should learn a lot from Japanese, Chinese and Vietnamese retail diplomacy which I also call **lifestyle diplomacy**. Their strategic marketing-challenged diplomacy in Washington DC has obviously not been a success but it is not late for them to come up to speed with the fast-paced demands of today's economic environment.

12. China was once loathed in America for supposedly being "communist." Not anymore. Most Americans now sleep in Chinese-made clothes on Chinese-made bedspreads under Chinese-made fans after watching sensational cable news on Chinese-made big screen TV sets and eating dinner made with Chinese-made spices and served with Chinese-made dish bowls or conveniently at nearby all-you-can-eat Chinese restaurants. Where is the fear of "communism" in all that? Nowhere! Japan was a World War II foe, and the Vietnam War claimed many American lives. These countries once had very negative image in America. Not anymore. If they could overcome, African countries like Nigeria could too.

13. The preconceived notion that everyone born on African soil is dumb or dubious certainly hampers business transactions between Black immigrants (including exporters) and many Americans. Unbeknown to their employers, many Americans employed in sales and customer service miss huge sales opportunities just because they can't stand Nigerian, Kenyan or Gambian accents. The funny "Africans are dumb" theory is radically disproved by the fact that many highly skilled professionals from African countries work in the health, education, IT and finance sectors of the American economy. A number of them have been elected to public offices. Many of them studying in American universities – from Harvard to University of Iowa - are proving their mettle. Former UN Secretary General and Nobel Peace laureate Kofi Annan from Ghana, Nobel Literature laureate Wole Soyinka from Nigeria, first environmentalist winner of Nobel Peace Prize and founder of the Green Belt Movement, Dr. Wangari Maathai of Kenya, and International statesman and Nobel Peace laureate Nelson Mandela of South Africa are certainly not dumb. Are they?

When I was articulating the foregoing views sometimes as late as 3am in the serene mid-western city of Coralville in Iowa, I had you in mind and I am honored that we finally met through the pages of this say-it-as-it-is book. By reading it all, you have indeed demonstrated your openness to spreading the wonder of objectivity about the real continent of Africa and I am deeply grateful.

Objectivity about issues and events relating to Africa has been one of the rarest commodities of our time, and because it has been very rare, trade and tourism have been adversely affected across the continent and millions of people – perhaps including you - and small businesses – perhaps including yours - have been denied the benefits of discovering and experiencing the real Africa. But I remain optimistic that things will change for the better, perhaps in my life-time.

Thank you so much for reading but remember, what is worth reading is worth sharing.

Afterword

An American should rightly be called an American, not a North American, and a Chinese should be called a Chinese, not an Asian. But should a Kenyan, Ghanaian, Gambian or Nigerian be called an African? That question forms the nominal backdrop for ***Don't Africa Me*** by C.P. Eze in which his interviewees provide interestingly differing answers.

When Eze told me he was writing ***Don't Africa Me***, a book showing how the geo-branding war on Africa has had a debilitating impact on trade and tourism in sub-Saharan African countries, I thought it was a square peg in a square hole, a good subject for a well informed writer like him.

He and I have had series of discussions in the past on a gamut of issues relating to globalization, personal re-branding and US-Nigeria relations that laid bare his interesting thrust of comparative analysis and impressive understanding of important global issues, which I think has a lot to do with his political science and journalism background and his wide travels.

Though some of his analyses and ideas in **Don't Africa Me** could be too hot to handle as some readers will discover, I agree with him that "Africa needs trade, not aid" is not just a new sleek slogan begging for media attention but a street-wise necessity borne out of the African continent's non-transformative experiences with insufficient Northern aid.

He goes on to express his candid opinion that many aid agencies and Africa-focused celebrities are not necessarily pleading the cause of the truly needy people in African countries but rather using the Help Africa Now Banner to re-brand themselves or boost their media visibility and brand value. He laments the expensive lifestyle of some senior aid workers in Africa who, according to him, put donations from compassionate Americans to wrong use, giving target beneficiaries a little to encourage them to pose for photographs or videos that would be used to raise more money in the US.

And while such pictures could attract more donations and make nonprofits and celebrities look good
on TV, they drive deeper the erroneous impression
that African nations are good for nothing other than
well promoted handouts. The author vigorously
challenges such impression, contending that the images fully serve to keep African countries as sources
of raw materials for big corporations not only in
America but also China, the country with the world's
largest foreign reserves which, he says, is propping
up the genocidal regime of Sudan.

He therefore lays the burden of strategically re-
branding African countries and pursing much-
needed development squarely on the shoulders of
the citizens (home and abroad) and governments of
such countries, supporting his position with ample
facts, figures and personal experiences.

In **Don't Africa Me,** the author makes no pretence
of his belief that many citizens and governments of
African countries are not fully discharging their re-
sponsibilities. Specifically, he took issues with many
of such citizens in America who change their accent
and stripe themselves of any visible sign of their
Ethiopianness, Nigerianness or Kenyanness thus
denying Americans the opportunity to associate their
highly skilled manpower as doctors, pharmacists,
nurses and software engineers to their countries of
birth. In contrast, people from Asian countries like
Korea, Vietnam and India retain their accents and

cultural outlook on life while collaborating with their compatriots to make a lot of money through very visible entrepreneurship. Statistics from the Census Bureau bears him out as Asians have the highest household income in the US.

Asian nations like China and India, he explained, have proven that international trade has the power to transform the lives that Northern aid has not been able to transform. These two very populous Asian countries wisely weighed their options, clearly understood their target markets, and came up with practical methodologies to propel their economic development and global reach and influence. They knew, of course, that nobody else would do it for them.

As the author opined, China, Japan and Vietnam all had bad image in America about three decades ago. China was seen through the prohibitive lens of "communism," Japan was a World War II foe while America had fought a long war in Vietnam that Americans still remember with mixed feelings or resentment. Yet, these three countries have successfully changed their image in America using what the author calls a blend of front porch and consumer product diplomacy.

Thus, while Americans see China, for instance, through the ubiquitous Chinese all-you-can-eat restaurants, Chinese movies featuring Jacky Chan and

Jet Li, and the innumerable affordable consumer products that Americans love, they see Nigeria through what the author aptly described as PIDIC (Poverty, Instability, Disease, Illiteracy and Corruption), which are not unique to any country or continent in the world. China became the world's factory while Nigeria, the fifth largest oil supplier to the US and home to the world's largest gas reserves, is still bleeding profusely from the wounds inflicted on it by advance fee fraud, a crime perpetrated by a very tiny segment of its 150 million people.

To the author, the challenge is for countries like Nigeria, Kenya and others to reinvent and reposition themselves in important markets like America following the examples of China, Japan and Vietnam that replaced, not repaired their image. Japan, for instance, forced the world to see it through its three best diplomats, Toyota, Honda and Sony, three strong global brands.

In all, *Don't Africa Me*, a book of compelling analysis and solutions, says African countries need to have palpable economic visibility in America to make meaningful impact in this century.

— **Councilman Kyrian Nwagwu,** First African-born elected official in State of Michigan

References/Notes

Chapter One: The PIDIC Syndrome

1. "Africa: Trade Can Revitalize Growth on Continent" by Obiageli Katryn Ezekwesili, World Bank's Vice President for Africa, This Day newspaper opinion, Lagos Nigeria, November 13, 2007, published on AllAfrica.com on November 14, 2007.

2. Peter M. Storment cited in "Nova Capital Partners Announces Investment in Nigeria's Intercontinental Bank," a press release by Nova Capital Partners, LLC, May 29, 2007, http://www.novacapitalpartners.com/media.html

3. "Intercontinental Bank Secures $50.5m Foreign Syndicated Facility," Daily Independent Online Edition, Monday, September 24, 2007

4. "My vision for Nigeria – Soludo" by Seun Ade-sida, Daily Sun, Monday, January 1, 2007

5. "Nigerian leaders 'stole' $380bn," BBC News, Friday, 20 October 2006, http://news.bbc.co.uk/2/hi/africa/6069230.stm

6. Human Rights Watch report on Nigeria, Volume 19, No. 16(A), October 2007. The sub-title of the report is Corruption and Poverty in Nigeria, http://hrw.org/reports/2007/nigeria1007/5.htm #_Toc179178223

7. "Chinese corruption 'astonishing,'" BBC News, Thursday, October 11, 2007, http://news.bbc.co.uk/2/hi/asia-pacific/7039383.stm

8. Judge Radhi Hamza al-Radhi, former commissioner of the Iraqi Commission on Public Integrity, cited in "Ex-Investigator Details Iraqi Corruption: He Tells House Panel That Maliki's Government Thwarted Probes" by Glenn Kessler, Washington Post Staff Writer, Friday, October 5, 2007; Page A16

9. "Chinese bridge collapse kills 36," BBC News, Wednesday, August 15 2007, http://news.bbc.co.uk/2/hi/asia-pacific/6945301.stm

10. "Zimbabwe: Tourist Arrivals Up Despite Deepening Political Crisis," Shame Makoshori, Financial Gazette Harare, September 26, 2007 – published online by AllAfrica.com on September 28, 2007. Since sit-tight President Robert Mugabe's controversial land re-distribution program that dispossessed Zimbabwe's White minority of most of the country's fertile lands and turned them over to the absolute Black majority, the southern Afrcan country has been under the captious eyes of the international media.

11. Ibid.

12. Ibid.

13. "Zimbabwe's nurses in exodus to Britain" in Daily Mail, September 22, 2007, www.dailymail.co.uk

14. "Africa ponders making trade work", BBC, Tuesday, 18 May, 2004

15. Africa Trade, World Bank, http://go.worldbank.org/KQMOOUVPX0

16. "Africa tackles trade dilemmas" by Orla Ryan, BBC, Sunday, 23 May, 2004

17. "Trading services: an opening or a noose? Africa puzzles over implications of trade talks in Ge-

neva" By Gumisai Mutume, Africa Recovery (a
UN publication now called Africa Renewal),
Vol.16#1, April 2002, page 26

Chapter Three: The surface is never deep

1. "Small Business Drives The U.S. Economy:
Provides Jobs For Over Half Of The Nation's Private
Workforce," News Release SBA Number: 05-
37-US ADVO, U.S. Small Business Administration, August 4, 2005

2. "Iraq Now Ranked Second Among World's
Failed States" by David Morgan, Reuters, Monday,
June 18, 2007

3. "FEATURE - Young Indian women march to
reclaim streets of fear" by Palash Kumar, Reuters,
Sunday, Oct 8, 2006.

Chapter Four: From virtual accents to verbal pity

1. "U.S. Census Bureau: Household Income Rises,
Poverty Rate Declines, Number of Uninsured

Up," US Census Bureau News, Tuesday August 28, 2007, www.census.gov

2. "Is Rwanda Ready for Paris? by Tina Dirmann, E! News, Tuesday, 25 Sep 2007

Chapter Five: Suspect media, 'distant' kins and Brand Africa

1. "Obama draws crowds on slum tour," BBC News, Sunday, 27 August 2006, news.bbc.co.uk/2/hi/africa/5290844.stm
2. "Koinange: Big guns, big oil collide in Nigeria" by Jeff Koinange, CNN, February 10, 2007
3. Ibid
4. Ibid
5. Robin Wright King, email response to C. Paschal Eze's email question, September 22, 2007. Robin Wright King, MBA, is author of the book, Papa Was A Rolling Stone: A Daughter's Journey to Forgiveness.

6. Ibid.

Chapter Six: Geo-branding shock and awe

1. "Beckham is down and out" by Grahame L. Jones and Jaime Cardenas, Los Angeles Times, August 31, 2007

Chapter Seven: What "communist" China taught us

1. "China's influence spread around world" article by William Foreman, Associated Press, September 2, 2007

2. David Zweig, professor at Hong Kong University of Science and Technology, quoted in "China's influence spread around world" by William Foreman, Associated Press, September 2, 2007. Zweig was quoted in William Foreman's article as saying, "the Chinese just want to trade their way to power" and "In the past, if a state wanted to expand, it had to take territory. You don't grab colonies anymore. You just need to have competitive goods to trade."

3. "Issues of Importance to American Business in the US-China Commercial Relationship," US Chamber of Commerce Report, September 2007

4. "From 'Made in China' to 'Invented in China'" CCTV, October 7, 2007, http://www.cctv.com/program/bizchina/200710 07/101460.shtml. CCTV is China's 24-hour English Language news channel covering the globe through six satellites. I watch it often in Iowa USA.

5. "China has 106 billionaires compared with only 15 last year," Shanghai (AFP), Wednesday, Octo-

ber 10, 2007,
http://news.yahoo.com/s/afp/20071010/lf_afp/
chinawealthbusinessbillionaireshu-
run_071010202701

6. "Issues of Importance to American Business in
the US-China Commercial Relationship," US
Chamber of Commerce Report, September 2007

7. "Critique of the Gotha Program," a letter by
Karl Marx in May 1875

8. "Phrases that defined a career: Some of
Reagan's most memorable lines" by Tom Curry,
MSNBC, June 5, 2004

9. "History of the Papacy" article on An-
swers.com,
http://www.answers.com/topic/history-of-the-
papacy#copyright

10. Ibid.

Chapter Eight: Dismantling Brand Africa

1. "Out of Africa: A Needed Surge of Exports to
Spur Growth, Cut Poverty," op-ed by World Bank
Africa Region Vice President Gobind Nankani,
http://go.worldbank.org/CWMEH117D0

References/Notes

2. "Foreign Investment, Remittances Outpace Debt As Sources Of Finance For Developing Countries," World Bank News Release No: 2003/266/S, Johannesburg April 7, 2003, http://go.worldbank.org/3JRKW3WO40

3. "Coltan trade funds DRC war – report," The Namibian, Wednesday, January 16, 2002. Democratic Republic of Congo (DRC) has the world's largest deposit of coltan used in making cell phones, among other things.

4. "Sudan, Iran find a bypass to U.N. sanctions" by Barbara Slavin, USA TODAY, June 10, 2007
5. "Africa Development Indicators 2007," International Bank for Reconstruction and Development/The World Bank Washington, D.C. U.S.A, October 2007

6. "Doing Business 2008: Making a Difference," International Finance Corporation website, http://ifc.org/ifcext/media.nsf/Content/Doing_Business_2008

7. "Ibrahim Index of African Governance: A Summary of The Rankings," http://www.moibrahimfoundation.org. Dr. Mo Ibrahim, Africa's telecommunication pioneer, is on a mission to promote governance on the continent.

8. "Mauritius Highest, Somalia Lowest on Africa Governance Index," NewsFeed Researcher,

179

http://newsfeedresearcher.com/data/articles_w39
/idw2007.09.25.13.22.50.html

9. "South Africa's 2010 Cup challenge," by Mohammed Allie, BBC News,
http://news.bbc.co.uk/2/hi/africa/5141582.stm

10. German Chancellor Angela Merkel, cited in "Merkel supports South Africa" (FIFA.com) Friday 5 October 2007. Merkel was German chancellor during the 2006 FIFA World Cup in Germany.

Bonus Chapter

Hot Internet tips and tools for exporters, importers

I must start by noting that the Internet is full of fraudsters and horrible accounts of unsuspecting fraud victims, which are part of the issues I deal with in my work as a certified e-commerce consultant. And because the Internet poses genuine trust and security questions and concerns, many people are uncomfortable and unfavorably disposed to it. Spam is as copious and annoying as calls from debt collectors. Identity theft is rife. Intellectual property theft abounds. Terrorists use the Internet to spread their messages of hate. Pedophiles are all over the cyberspace wreaking havoc. Criminals open phony ephemeral charity fundraising sites and defraud unsuspecting donors or set up flashy cybermalls and disappear as soon as they get lots of money in their drag nets. The list goes on and on.

Still a great asset

Despite the aforementioned credibility and security issues and concerns over the Internet, I still give it many thumbs up for the simple reasons that:

A. it is accessible to millions of people around the world, including those in African countries like Nigeria and Gambia where there are many Internet cafes;

B. it is present in many homes and offices around the world, including those of African countries like Ghana and South Africa, especially in middle class and elite circles;

C. most US, Canadian and British public libraries offer free one-hour-per-day Internet browsing to users, meaning the poor and the jobless in Detroit, Waterloo or Washington DC and those who don't see the Internet as a basic need are not left out;

D. it is dynamic enough to capture socio-political and economic events and issues up to the minute;

E. it makes information dissemination a participatory and non-exclusive affair – blogs, wikipedia, ebooks, Squidoo.com, etc;

F. talking about blogs, they make it easy to expose hypocritical politicians and corporate executives shielded or surface-scratched by the corporate media;

G. the Internet provides an easy way to "check people out" by Googling them – employers, journalists and new social or business contacts do it;

H. a basic 3-8 page website can be created in a day by a home business owner or rookie exporter in Accra or Abuja using cookie cutter site builders provided by most web hosting companies like ixwebhosting.com and siteground.com;

I. anybody, any organization, any country can run a wide-reaching advert campaign online with a small budget using Google Adwords (http://adwords.google.com/select/Login), for instance;

J. the impact of a website or an Internet campaign is easily measurable through web visitor statistics that help web owners and webmasters ascertain who visited, when and how and their conversion rate;

K. the trendy convergence online makes it easy to listen to audio and watch videos as well as upload, download or share them almost anywhere;

L. the Internet has become very interactive, very engaging and very crowd-driven that with simple "prosumer" cameras and cheap video editing software like Ulead Video Studio or Easy Media Creator 10, obscure youths have become icons almost overnight, with their messages reaching millions around the world;

M. the Internet is very helpful in product and service research before purchase – customer reviews, star ratings, product information, etc;

N. many people conveniently buy products and services online using Buy.com, Amazon.com, eBay.com, Elance.com, Getafreelancer.com, etc;

O. many people conveniently make or receive payments online using Paypal (https://www.paypal.com), for instance;

P. many people conveniently monitor their bank accounts online or simply bank online and often get higher interest rates using HSBC (http://www.hsbcusa.com), for instance;

Q. Many businesses have found the Internet very useful in providing customer support – live chat, contact forms, Frequently Asked Questions page, ticket management tools, etc;

R. Voice over Internet Protocol (VoIP) or Voice over Broadband has made local, national and international phone calls very affordable – Skype.com, Vonage.com, Packet8.net, etc. Skype, for instance, is used from Jos to Johannesburg.

For those reasons, I strongly believe exporters and importers everywhere and especially in African nations like Kenya, Botswana, South Africa, Nigeria and Mauritius need to make better and wider use of the Internet in better promoting their various manufactured products as well as services.

The Internet is also a handy tool in directly facilitating exports as many Chinese globally thinking entrepreneurs do with sites like CyberImports.com.cn. Its owner, Cyber Imports, represents over 2000 Chinese factories. There is also the b2b website, Ecvv.com, which said it had 1 million registered members, 2 million catalogs, 1 million daily visits and over half a million buyers from 220 countries and territories around the world as at June 2007. Ecvv.com is a great place to find Chinese exporters.

Why shouldn't entrepreneurs from African countries like Nigeria, Ghana, Kenya or Mauritius have b2b, export promotion and facilitation websites as robust, user-friendly, well promoted and well visited as **Ecvv.com, Kompass.com or Alibaba.com**?

"Brand Africa implies that people in African countries have no Internet access or need for it. Fortunately, they do."

May be, they are discouraged by the fact that Brand Africa implies that people in African countries have no Internet access or need for it. Fortunately, they do. In this post-modern information age, they must have Internet access like nations in other parts of the world. Fortunately, there are many middle class homes with Internet connection, and Internet cafes are booming businesses in cities across Africa. I have seen and used Internet cafes in some African cities. My office computer when I was working in the West African country of Republic of The Gambia had good Internet connection. Almost all leading African businesses I can think of have Internet presence though I place more value on Internet prowess consequent upon powerful sales copy starting with captivating value proposition, smooth navigation, dynamic interactivity and high organic traffic from major search engines like Google.com, Yahoo.com, Live.com, Ask.com and Excite.com.

Most, if not all, African governments have their own websites. However, many of them are not easily navigable, professionally optimized for major search engines, very interactive, podcast-providing and emotionally tuned to target visitors, and are therefore not as globally visible, properly positioned and effectively communicating as they ought to be in the web 2.0 era. Many newspapers, magazines and TV stations across Africa have their own news websites as well and some of them send feeds to pan-African news sites like AllAfrica.com which are popular among "Africans in the Diaspora" but need strong cross-over appeal.

Getting free Internet publicity is easier than you think

Yahoo! News, Google News and Topix.com are popular leaders in online news which provides great "get-the-word-out" opportunities for all exporters and importers.

African countries and their many universities, and hospitality and tourism businesses will also find online news portals very useful and rewarding, which is why they should ensure timely eye-popping news about their unique research findings, export-friendly product launches, breakthroughs, tourism promotions, unusual events and so on appear on them regularly.

Here are **free press release distribution websites** you could submit your quality, news-rich, search engine optimized press releases to:

A. Prweb.com – sends feeds to Google News
B. Openpr.com – sends feeds to Google News
C. Prfree.com
D. Pressbox.co.uk

E. USprwire.com – sends feeds to Google News, Topix

F. Clickpress.com – sends feeds to Google News, Topix

G. Prleap.com – sends feeds to Google News

H. 24-7pressrelease.com

I. Prlog.org

J. Prbuzz.com

K. Pressmethod.com

L. Newswiretoday.com – sends feeds to Google News

M. Express-press-release.com

N. Free-press-release.com

O. TheOpenPress.com

I do a good number of my best Internet publicity campaigns using these well visited, RSS technology-friendly press release distribution sites. A number of them send feeds to Google News, Topix and other powerful news aggregators which is really good for wider global reach. Some of them will tell you how many times your press release was clicked or emailed so you can assess its impact, which is very important. Some of them allow you to upload pictures and even videos, which enhance the value, attractiveness and effectiveness of your press release. But note that the success of your press release depends a lot on whether it is search engine optimized, whether your title is captivating, whether your information is relevant and timely, whether it is simple, short and sweet and whether it has link to your site and your contact information.

I also recommend RSS directories like feeds2read.net, feedfury.com and outpost-earth.com especially for daily export/import columns and product blogs that deserve wider Internet visibility.

> *"...there are many people around the world who are curious to know the truth about you and your export products, for instance, and they easily turn to the Internet."*

This is important because, as you can imagine, there are many people around the world who are curious to know the truth about you and your export products, for instance, and they easily turn to the Internet. There are also many people who are curious to know the truth about Africa, but finding nothing really helpful in the corporate media, tend to turn to the increasingly people-powered Internet. As I wrote in my article titled *Surefire way to get business publicity*, "There has been a paradigm shift in PR, and it has to do with online press release syndication using Really Simple Syndication (RSS) technology. Today's PR is

Internet-driven, and it is cost-effective and convenient. 98% of journalists use Internet daily; 92% to research for articles, 76% to find new sources, experts like you, 73% to find press releases like yours. Yes, quality press releases like yours, according to Middleberg/Ross Survey." **(1)**

About 26 million Americans used the Internet daily for news in August 2006. Surveys by The Pew Research Center for the People and the Press have shown that more Americans are now turning to the Internet for news. The Center put the figure at 31%, a 2% increase from 2004 to 2006. Within the two year period, the percentage of Americans who regularly watched cable TV news dipped from 38% to 34%, while that of nightly network news dipped as well from 34% to 28%. There was also a drop in newspaper readership and percentage of radio listeners.

I remember running a Best Caring Author campaign exclusively on the Internet in early 2007. Three major American newspapers, Atlanta Journal Constitution in Georgia, Wichita Eagle in Kansas and Detroit Free Press in Michigan, published stories on it, without me emailing, mailing or faxing journalists or broadcasters, paying a publicist or placing an expensive ad. I simply posted my press release on My-BookNews.com, a user-friendly press release syndication site, and voila! My campaign achieved its purpose, at least in the short run.

> *"One often ignored way to capture the attention and interest of people in the North is by focusing on things they are passionate about."*

One often ignored way to capture the attention and interest of people in the North is by focusing on things they are passionate about. For instance, there are very many pet lovers in America, Canada, Germany, United Kingdom and Australia, with many of them turning to the Internet for information and products on pet training and clothing, among others. Thus, properly optimized, very interactive and picture-rich customizable **pet clothing sites with sufficient product descriptions and very competitive pricing could prove very valuable** in generating huge revenues and much-needed awareness about sub-Saharan African countries.

Nationals of these countries living from Detroit and Vancouver to London and Frankfurt should find in such sites good and beckoning business opportunities. Americans, for instance, spend over $30 billion annually on pets. Americans are passionate about their pets, and according to a Yahoo/MediaVest study on harnessing the power of Internet consumers' passion, "Over half, 53 percent, would try a new brand if it was associated with their passion, compared with 41 percent of typical users." **(2)** If that is not a yawning net begging for smart goal scorers, I don't what is.

Go on and spread the hidden wonder online

I believe small and medium sized businesses with export or import operations and African countries like Nigeria and Kenya are better off with the Internet than with many corporate media giants that have proven they have an axe to grind with them. It could be cheaper and certainly more effective to run a well timed, several months long, and very accessible pay-per-click campaign on Google, Yahoo or MSN than to place a full page ad in New York Times or a 30-second ad on CNN. A MySpace account may prove more effective in telling an African country's story of attractive trade and tourism opportunities than a high profile Black-Tie, long-speech event in Washington DC. The same is true of YouTube, which provides a great platform for African countries to broadcast themselves.

MySpace and YouTube have tens of millions of members and users, many of whom are seemingly open-minded, adventurous and impressionable. I believe African countries, especially those interested in significantly boosting their international tourist arrivals, should fully embrace the outgoing, full-loving, global village conscious MySpace and You-Tube generation that are more likely to try Made-in-Nigeria or Made-in-Namibia goods or tourism products than those in the New York Times or Washington Post generation. Though the latter are more financially stable and comfortable, they are less adventurous and more status quo-minded than the former.

> *"...the Internet offers African countries from South Africa to Ethiopia and the many businesses operating in them the platform to tell their own stories in an engaging way to an information hungry world that has been told all the bad things in Africa but denied information on all the good things therein."*

As one report put it, "Americans downloaded more than 9 billion videos during the month of July, primarily from Google sites. Google video platforms accounted for more than 2.5 billion (27%) streams during the counting period, most of those clips were watched via YouTube." **(3)** So, though MySpace and YouTube present genuine concerns over cyber pedophiles, cyber terrorists and semi-nudists, I submit that the Internet offers small and medium sized exporters and importers around the world but especially those from African countries from South Africa to Ethiopia the platform to tell their own stories in an engaging way to an information hungry world that has been told all the bad things in Africa but denied information on all the good things therein like quality manufactured products and rich tourism products.

A 2005 iCrossing report showed that "Books, movies and music are the most popular items to purchase online across all demographics (gender, age, and income). Travel and clothes/apparel are the next most popular categories, with roughly equal percents purchasing them online." **(4)** These are all items that run from Ghana to Kenya.

So, I fervently encourage the publication of more fact-based and professionally designed Amazon-listed books, including ebooks and audio books, on the realities of African societies, and better marketing and wider distribution of Nigeria's Nollywood movies and thousands of sweet sounding tunes from across Africa using Amazon.com, eBay.com, Buy.com, CDBaby.com, Barnesandnoble.com, Target, Wal-Mart and others. People of sub-Saharan Africa – living therein or across the Northern Hemisphere - need to tell their own story in an emotionally connecting way because others have told it for too long with venom and pounds of flesh, others have told it for too long in ways that make objectivity a matter of incarcerated imagination.

> *"People of sub-Saharan Africa – living therein or across the Northern Hemisphere - need to tell their own story in an emotionally connecting way because others have told it for too long with venom and pounds of flesh..."*

But come to think of it, the individuals and corporate and nonprofit organizations telling such stories do not bear the whole blame. Many things in life abhor half-measures, vacuums and insouciance and branding is one of them. I either clearly and consistently tell (and remind) people who I am, what I stand for and how I am best positioned to help solve their problems and meet their aspirations or others will gladly concoct something terrible about me, trumpet it unflinchingly on roof tops and people will conveniently believe them.

You are either proactive about your relevance and distinctive qualities or defensively reactionary about them because others will easily and enthusiastically fill in the blanks and hurt your feelings and fortunes.

This happens too often in politics, interpersonal relations, local business and trade and tourism especially because people tend to believe whoever shouts the loudest and longest, they tend to honor the first and fastest.

South Africa, for instance, is big on Information Technology, and I think it can draw a lot of inspiration from the examples set by countries like China, India, Romania and Russia in the marketing and sales of both customized and cookie-cutter software. Their savvy entrepreneurs at home and abroad flooded the Internet with international marketplaces where software developers bid for jobs from people around the world in need of custom software. Do a Google search for "custom software development," "outsourcing software development" and "freelance software developers" and see for yourself. Lots of money have been flowing into countries like China, India, Romania, Bulgaria and Russia as a result, and that's what I think the Internet can help African countries achieve.

> *I remember how difficult it was for me to get pictures of what I call "the other Africa" on the Internet..."*

I remember how difficult it was for me to get pictures of what I call "the other Africa" on the Internet for my PowerPoint presentation on "Turn off your TV and see Africa." I found appreciable number of free and non-free pictures on exotic wildlife, rural squalor and urban filth but very, very few of boulevards, Internet cafes, impressive university buildings, global hotel brands, high rise buildings, stock exchanges, manufacturing plants, product manufacturing process, living rooms of average city dwellers, product launches, tarred roads and street lights, night sky, sandy beeches, top flight restaurants, beautiful tarmacs and runways, legislative buildings and presidential mansions, children's playgrounds, theme parks, and so on.

These are the kind of images that will help to counter the notion in countries of the North that Africa – a continent of 54 sovereign nations – is a big jungle or heap of ruins, which certainly puts off many prospective tourists, investors and importers. Many Americans still prove the aphorism that a picture speaks a thousand words.

When some people with objective polycentric worldview find a TV or newspaper report on an African country appalling, they should find not only factual texts but also pictures that present an objective view of the African country on the Internet. The same is also true of people who want to find out if their winter vacation could be best spent in an exotic African destination or elsewhere.

The Internet is usually their first port of call but if they find nothing compelling from African destinations like Ghana, Gambia and Seychelles, they are likely to make their decisions based on usually negative Brand Africa-geared information from other sources. According to Pew Internet and American Life Project, "Our surveys show that 45% of internet users, or about 60 million Americans, say that the internet helped them make big decisions or negotiate their way through major episodes in their lives in the previous two years." **(5)**

It is certainly not the duty of prospects in the North to come to African countries like Nigeria and South Africa to take pictures and make them available online to millions of people around the world. It is the duty of citizens, businesses and governments of African countries. If they fail to rise up to this duty, and provide members of the world community with the information they need, others will fill the resultant vacuum with their biases. The information age abhors vacuum.

Studies have found that many consumers in countries like America depend on the Internet not only for product research but also actual purchases. For instance, a September 2007 report by iCrossing based on a survey conducted by Opinion Research

Corporation titled "How America Searches," found, among other things, that:

- American consumers are shopping online now more than ever: percentage of online adults who reported making a purchase online at least monthly increased from 30% in 2005 to 39% in 2007;

- As many as 42% of all consumers see information about brands and products on sites like Wikipedia as extremely or very influential on their online purchase decisions, while blogs, YouTube videos and brand profiles on social networking sites carry significant weight with shoppers aged 18-to-44;

- Customer reviews grow in importance: Use of customer product reviews and evaluations to research online purchases jumped from 40% in 2005 to 49% in 2007; 41% of all online shoppers say they always or often consult consumer reviews before making a purchase decision, and 70% cite them as extremely or very important factors in their decision-making process;

- More shoppers turning to emerging online research tools: Shopping comparison sites, online image search and blogs now capture a larger share of shoppers during the research phase of the purchase process, with the percentage of those consulting blogs more than doubling in the past two years; and

- **65% of online shoppers** conduct product research using search engines and the percentage of those searching around actual purchasing – finding on- and offline retailers – rose significantly between 2005 and 2007. **(6)**

Such findings are very helpful in fashioning out marketing strategies for penetrating and succeeding in the huge American market.

Some helpful sites for search engine optimization:

http://www.nichebot.com/v2/o/ − gives you 100 top keyword listings, competition results as well as number of times searched.

http://www.keywordspy.com/ - for keyword database, and monitoring your competitors' Internet marketing strategies.

http://www.ranks.nl/tools/spider.html - helps you find with your keyword density and prominence.

http://www.scrubtheweb.com/ - helps you find out if your website is search engine friendly.

http://www.widexl.com/remote/search-engines/metatag-analyzer.html - great tool for meta tag analysis. It also helps you see how your site would appear on search engines, and keywords to use in your meta tags, times found and density.

https://adwords.google.com/select/KeywordToolExternal - helps you find good keywords for your site or for your Google Adwords campaign.

Some other useful tools:

www.register.com – search to see if a domain name you are considering is available. Your domain name could help in your search engine ranking if it is composed of your major keyword like "Gambiafishexports.com" or "Ghanajewelryexports.com"

www.blogger.com,   www.wordpress.com, www.livejournal.com – for free blogs. Blogs have a wide readership, depending, of course, on their contents.

http://add.yahoo.com/fast/help/us/news/cgi _submitsource
- to recommend a news source to Yahoo! News.

http://www.google.com/support/news/bin/re quest.py - to recommend a news source to Google News.

http://www.kompass.com – to find export products/services and companies.

http://www.export.gov – helps US owned and operated companies export goods internationally.

http://www.buyusa.gov/home/ - helps American companies find international business partners worldwide, and companies outside the US - in countries like South Africa and Sierra Leone - find American suppliers of products and services.

http://www.fsis.usda.gov/regulations_&_polici es/Import_Information/index.asp - useful information for companies desiring to export meat, poultry and egg products to the US.

http://www.ic.gc.ca/epic/site/ic1.nsf/en/hom e - very helpful information on Canadian authentication and certification procedures, products and services pursuant to a fair marketplace.

http://www.agoa.gov/eligibility/product_eligib ility.html - to find out if your export product is AGOA eligible.

It should be kept in mind that the Internet is both a marketing and a sales tool. So, a website should be able to attract the attention of its target audience like vacation seeking Americans, create awareness about a tourism or export product, arouse interest of the target audience having been made aware of the tourism or export product, and propel such action as calling to get more information or pointing the cursor at **"Click here now to book your vacation" or "Click to buy this quality pet hat."**

Notes/References:

1. "Surefire way to get business publicity" by Paschal Eze, www.PaschalEzeMedia.com/ businesspublicity.html

2. "An anatomy of a passionista" by Helen Leggatt in BizReport, October 1, 2007, http://www.bizreport.com/2007/10/an_anatomy _of_a_passionista.html. The article is based on a new research by Yahoo and MediaVest on harnessing the power of Internet brand advocates.

3. "US users consumed 3 hours of online video in July," an article by Kristina Knight in BizReport.com, September 13, 2007, http://www.bizreport.com/2007/09/us_users_co nsumed_3_hours_of_online_video_in_july.html

4. "How America Searches: Online Shopping," iCrossing October 2005 Report

5. "The Internet's Growing Role in Life's Major Moments" by Pew Internet and American Life Project, April 19, 2006

6. "How America Searches: Online Retail," a report by iCrossing, Inc. based on a survey conducted by Opinion Research Corporation, September 2007,

http://www.icrossing.com/articles/How%20Ame
rica%20Searches%20-%20Online%20Retail.pdf

Printed in the United States
142226LV00002B/27/P

9 780980 076806